THE LAND
QUESTION
AND EUROPEAN
SOCIETY
SINCE 1650

THE LAND
QUESTION
AND EUROPEAN
SOCIETY
SINCE 1650

FRANK E. HUGGETT

with 84 illustrations

HARCOURT BRACE JOVANOVICH, INC.

Frontispiece 'May labour be rewarded with success.' A modest hope of self-sufficiency was the age-old dream of many peasants, but all too often they had to battle against political, economic and natural obstacles which no amount of work could overcome.

Picture research by Alla Weaver

© 1975 THAMES AND HUDSON LTD, LONDON

First American edition 1975

ISBN 0-15-549005-2

Library of Congress Catalog Card Number: 75-788

PRINTED AND BOUND IN GREAT BRITAIN BY
JARROLD AND SONS LTD, NORWICH

CONTENTS

INTRODUCTION

Most histories of Europe, written as they usually are by members of the urban middle class, tend to concentrate on the growth of towns, the rise of industry and developments in urban politics and culture, treating the countryside and its inhabitants as an unchanging background against which the drama of European history was played out. This volume takes a different approach. Until the middle of the nineteenth century, or even later, most Europeans were country-dwellers who derived their livelihood from the land. About half of the French labour force was still engaged in agriculture in 1850; 45 per cent of the Germans were classified as agricultural workers in 1871; and over half of the Swedes, Norwegians and Danes remained peasants or farm workers to the end of the century. Even in the 1930s about 82 per cent of the working population in Bulgaria, 80 per cent in Rumania and Yugoslavia, 75 per cent in Poland, 60 per cent in Hungary and 40 per cent in Czechoslovakia were still employed on the land. The drift from the land was slow: almost a quarter of the working population of the European Economic Community was still employed in agriculture in 1958. Unless we take these people and their problems and aspirations into account, our historical perspective will be seriously out of focus. To neglect the farmer, the peasant and the agricultural worker is to remain ignorant about the vast majority of the men and women who have ever lived in Europe.

Nor can agriculture be brushed aside as something of historical importance, but of no immediate concern. The German peasantry and the agricultural slump in the inter-war period were important factors in Hitler's rise to power. Agriculture has been one of the most intractable problems for the Soviet leadership, while the Common Agricultural Policy has produced some of the greatest strains within the European Economic Community. Since the end of the Second World War, the increasing industrialization of farming and its much greater dependence on fossil fuels and their by-products have created new problems whose full significance has not yet been generally realized. The great reversal in the traditional balance between town and country has also caused increasing concern among environmentalists, ecologists and planners. Agricultural change, from time immemorial, has affected the way in which people live and their social, economic, political and cultural attitudes: it is not merely of antiquarian interest.

Because rural history has been so grossly neglected until very recent times, there are many topics, some of them ideally suited for computerized study, which still await their historians: diet and demography; international trade in farm produce and the international diffusion of agricultural techniques and ideas; the influence of the Church; the vital local histories which are so scarce, especially for the south; European sharecropping, from *mezzadria* in Italy through *métayage* in France to some steel-bow tenancy in Scotland. But the immense amount of detailed research which has been carried out in the post-war years by a new generation of historians with expanded sympathies has already enabled us to gain a much clearer picture of what happened in the countryside. The present volume tries to show how changes in land tenure, innovations in agricultural techniques, new methods of farming and the impact of industry and the towns have affected the patterns of European society in the modern period of history.

In seventeenth-century Europe, below the thin privileged crust of
kings and courtiers, bishops and abbots, nobility and gentry, judges
and officials, town regents and country squires, below Peter Laslett's
'one-class society',[1] there was another full and living world of untitled
people, lacking any prefix to their names. Some members of this
undistinguished majority worked as shopkeepers, artisans and servants in the cities and towns, but the greatest number were to be found
in hamlets and villages and on farms scattered throughout the European countryside, engaged in a multiplicity of rural tasks – the goat-
herd and the swineherd, the shepherd and the grazier, the ploughman
and the milkmaid, but above all the common peasant and the serf. In
the middle of the seventeenth century, well over three-quarters of the
total working population of Europe was employed in agriculture,
which still remained the fundamental basis of national prosperity.
'We are hung upon it by the teeth,'[2] wrote James Harrington, the
English political philosopher, in 1656.

Without the peasants, the gentlemen would have had to soil their
hands or starve; but dependence is no cause for love. Throughout
history the peasants have been the most maligned, the most exploited
and, until very recent times, the most misunderstood of all social
groups. Attitudes towards them have oscillated according to their
willingness or their refusal to accept the task assigned to them by high
society of providing services on demesnes, estates and roads, horses for
officials and cartage for lords, rents for landlords, taxes for kings,
tithes for clergymen and human fodder for the ceaseless wars. In
medieval times, priests and poets sometimes represented the peasants
as humble, hard-working, God-fearing benefactors of mankind,[3] but
more often they were seen as 'coarse and clumsy blockheads'.[4] Few
seventeenth-century gentlemen would have disagreed with the
verdict of Charles Loyseau, a French magistrate, that they were all
'base persons'.[5] It is an opinion which has persisted throughout much
of Europe to the present day. The friendlier words of some later

9

2, 3 The traditional view of the countryside as an unchanging background
to history: *above*, sixteenth-century milkmaid by Lucas van Leyden; *below*,
seventeenth-century swineherd, after David Teniers.

4 Adriaen Brouwer, *Peasants quarrelling over cards*: a graphic illustration of the attitude of superior classes, who viewed the peasants as 'base persons'.

writers – of Adam Smith, the British economist, of Prince Kropotkin, the Russian anarchist, of Björnstjerne Björnson, the Norwegian novelist and playwright – have been largely ignored, so that the peasant has come down through history as backward, cunning, greedy, sly. In Roget's *Thesaurus* he makes his entrance beside the boor, the tyke, the clown, the clodhopper, the yokel, the hick, the rube, the bog-trotter, the bumpkin and the chawbacon.

From about the twelfth to the fourteenth century high society in many parts of Europe smiled, a little coldly and a little wanly perhaps, upon the peasantry. There had never been so great and sustained a demand for their services as there was then with the expansion of the frontiers of Europe to the south and to the east and, probably, a relatively rapid rise in the population in the west. Beyond the Elbe, monasteries, princes and the Order of Teutonic Knights wooed German and other west European peasants out to their huge estates by offering them farms of reasonable size on favourable leases, and often granting them exemption from taxation for a number of years. In the south of Europe, too, there were new lands to be colonized after the collapse of the Spanish Caliphate in 1030 began to weaken the Moorish grip on Spain and Portugal. The Christian kingdoms in the north and east drove back the Moors, steadily though not without some set-backs, to the south. Toledo was taken in 1085, Lisbon in 1147, Cordoba in 1236 and Seville in 1248, confining the Moors to the small kingdom of Granada in the south. Huge tracts of land, which had been reconquered after many centuries of infidel occupation, were granted by the kings of Portugal, Castile and Aragon to military and monastic orders; but to attract settlers, autonomous municipalities were set up in Spain with special rights and privileges in the towns and the surrounding countryside. Many serfs in the north of Italy were freed during the great age of the communes, as in Bologna in 1257, where six thousand serfs were transformed into free *contadini*, provided with land and fixed assets for their farms by the citizens of the towns in return for half the produce. It seems possible, though we do not know for certain, that in the first flush of enthusiasm for this generally progressive attempt to forge more beneficial links between the countryside and the towns the citizens may have been more willing to make the necessary investments in the land than many of them were in later ages.

On the mainland of north-west Europe, the fairly general decay of the manorial system of farming during the twelfth and thirteenth centuries released many peasants from labour services on their lord's demesne, which they had performed with increasing reluctance; the services were commuted to money rents. Peasant services were in demand for what Marc Bloch has called 'the age of large-scale land clearance'[6] in the broad-leaved mixed oak forests of north-west and central Europe from the middle of the eleventh to the middle of the thirteenth century. New farms and villages were created in the former wastelands to satisfy the land-hunger of the growing population. During the same period some clearances were also made in the Mediterranean region, though a larger amount of the original open forest of evergreen oaks and pines had probably been cleared many centuries earlier in classical times with fire and axe and, at much greater ecological cost, by goats and sheep.

It was not all light and brightness in the peasant world, however, for that happy state was probably always to be found far more in folk-tales than in reality. Early in the fourteenth century the expansion of the preceding centuries came to a halt and an agricultural depression set in. Marginal land, including some that had only recently been re-claimed, was abandoned. In England, where they had persisted longer than in many continental countries, labour services were increased or reimposed, causing sporadic risings which culminated in the Peasants' Revolt of 1381. In newly reconquered lands like Spain and in many feudal areas, territorial lords tried to impose taxes and monopolies of mill, bakery and wine-press on the peasants, whether free or servile; and all peasants were subject to the common scourges of famine, war, pestilence and disease. In the fourteenth century isolated outbreaks of the plague culminated in the widespread, though not ubiquitous, Black Death of 1347–51, which killed millions of peasants. It is esti-mated that it took the small Norwegian population more than two centuries to regain all the land that had reverted to scrub and forest after the plague, carried to Bergen in an English ship, robbed so many farms of their occupants. The Hundred Years War, according to one contemporary chronicler, left large parts of France so devastated that 'neither cock crowed nor hen clucked'.[7]

For a time, however, it had seemed just possible that societies of relatively free and independent peasants, owing nothing but just and unresented tributes to their masters, might have flourished, not every-where in Europe, but certainly in many places. It was not to be. The peasant wanted to own or to have the right to use on reasonable terms enough land to provide subsistence for himself and for his family and to cater for their future welfare and their needs. (This has never, as far as can be seen, prevented the peasant from growing other crops for sale, exchange or barter: 'It is as habitual with peasants in many areas to grow two crops as to walk on two feet,' Daniel Thorner has written.[8]) The amount of land a peasant needed varied greatly from place to place and from century to century. It changed with the size of his family, the local environment, the kind of farming and the level of agricultural technology, the skill and industry of the peasant him-self and other variables. The amount could be increased by the taxes, tithes and tributes he was forced to provide, so that in parts of seven-teenth-century France these, plus necessary working expenses, doubled the necessary area; it could be diminished by the peasant's willingness to accept a lower standard of living for himself and his family, or by the opportunity to work part-time at some other trade, such as weaving or clock-making, or to supply produce for the market. The land question is the essential thread linking the whole of peasant history together: a sufficiency of land remained as essential to the peasant as the native air that he breathed.

5 *The Ploughman and Death*, by Hans Holbein the Younger. 'By the sweat of your brow you earn your meagre living. After long and wearisome labour, Death invites you to be his guest.'

A la fueur de ton uifaige
Tu gaigneras ta pauure uie.
Apres long trauail, & ufaige,
Voicy la Mort qui te conuie.

It was for this ideal that the peasant suffered, yet for the great majority it proved to be an elusive dream. There was an inherent contradiction in the peasant position. In non-industrial societies, lacking any methods of birth control but personal restraint, peasant success in feeding a growing population could only lead, in areas of partible inheritance, to subdivided plots incapable of providing a basic subsistence, and, in areas of primogeniture, to an increase in the number of the landless. By the middle of the seventeenth century, the growth of population in western Europe had already forced many peasants out of Swiss valleys to work as landless labourers on the plains below, or to serve as mercenaries in the armies of those foreign powers from whom their ancestors had succeeded in wresting their freedom three centuries or more before. It had driven some peasants further north in Norway to more inhospitable regions with shorter growing seasons.

6 Throughout history, peasants provided a source of cheap labour for the rich, who lived in huge castles and châteaux.

7 Peasants ploughing their own small divided plots in fifteenth-century France.

It had left the scar of many a transitory hoe or plough upon barren hillside, moor or heath.

A relative scarcity of land, however, was also produced by other factors, including the level of investment; ownership; and the way in which the land was farmed and used. In the south of Europe the vast unimproved estates, the ravages of goat and sheep, the low level of investment and the inherent difficulties of climate and terrain had produced a largely artificial shortage. In the north-west of Europe, by the middle of the seventeenth century, the greed of autocratic kings for taxes to finance their wars, and the rise of new lords who had learnt their skills in counting-house and law-court, had already deprived some peasants of their land and had made it difficult for many more to subsist on their smallholdings. In eastern Europe land was abundant, but labour scarce; as a result, most of the peasant settlers had been deprived of their freedom and forced to labour on their lord's estates for many days each year in a new and sometimes brutal form of serfdom.

These changes had been brought about gradually over the centuries, usually at the village level, where all agrarian history must first be studied. But, in very broad terms, divergent attitudes towards the peasantry had developed in the west of Europe and in the east. The general view of high society in western Europe was neatly summarized by Gustav Bonde, the seventeenth-century Swedish statesman: 'It is better to milk the cow than to hit it over the head.'[9] In eastern Europe, however, the latter method was favoured. It was a fateful choice which was to take the two parts of Europe along very different rural paths and was to be fraught with consequence for the development of their respective societies.

The process of enserfment in the east of Europe was slow, being imposed first at the local level and ratified nationally only later. Hungary was an exception. There, in the thirteenth century, peasants in the frontier region had been 'ennobled'[10] – that is, freed from taxation – in return for guarding the borders against invaders; but when an army of peasant crusaders turned against their lords in 1514, the peasantry with some exceptions was bound to 'real and perpetual servitude'.[11] Although this servitude did not last for eternity as the Hungarian nobles had planned, it did continue for almost three and a half centuries. 'History', says Dénes Sinor, 'probably knows of no legislation more shameful.'[12] Peasants were deprived of freedom of movement; they were forced to pay considerable taxes; and at least one lord had all his peasants branded like cattle.

The history of peasants in east Germany took a different course. The growth of an increasingly profitable trade in grain to western Europe, particularly to the Netherlands, made the lords eager to expand their own estates. The Order of Teutonic Knights was seriously weakened by a Polish defeat in 1410, which enabled the lords to usurp some of its judicial and administrative functions. Their control of local courts and of credit enabled them to whittle away the peasants' freedom. Here, one peasant who was in debt had most of his land confiscated; there, another peasant who had leased land on the lord's demesne had his rent replaced by labour services. Between the fifteenth century and the middle of the seventeenth, the vast majority of peasants were transformed into serfs. They were forbidden to leave their smallholdings and forced to work on the lord's estates for a fixed maximum wage, while their daughters were obliged to marry peasants who lived on the estates to ensure a continuity and an increase in the future labour supply.

An even more extreme form of serfdom gradually developed in Russia from the end of the sixteenth century or even before. The causes are still debated by historians, but some of the main reasons seem to have been the labour shortages caused on many estates by peasants fleeing to settle new land in the east and the south-east conquered by Muscovite Russia from the Mongols; the granting of land confiscated from the old aristocracy and of Crown estates to the new class of gentry who led the tsar's troops; and the increased demand for grain to feed the armies and the growing towns. Even earlier, however, at the end of the fifteenth century, peasant tenants were allowed by law to leave their lord's estates to farm elsewhere only during a short period every autumn. In a vast expanding country with a relatively small population, there is always a labour problem: the runaway peasant was throughout history one of the Russian lord's main concerns. The period of time during which peasants could be recaptured and brought back to the lord's estate was gradually extended, from five years towards the end of the sixteenth century to ten years in 1642. Finally, in 1649, a code of laws was promulgated which bound 90 per cent of the peasants and all the members of their families irrevocably to their lord. Only death or their lord's permission could end this attachment, for if a peasant escaped, even to a foreign country, there was no limit to the period in which he could be captured. The code allowed torture to be used to extract confessions if children denied their relationship to their parents. These laws marked the start of a long debasement of the mass of the Russian peasantry into a beaten, tortured and deprived race of subjects, increasingly indistinguishable from slaves (though the fiction of their legal personality was preserved), who were sold like cattle at public auction.

There was no parallel to this large-scale human bondage in the older-established countries of western Europe, where many of the former serfs had gained their freedom during the Middle Ages. Serfdom in a milder form lingered on in isolated cases in England until the seventeenth century, and in some parts of the Continent to an even later period, so that there were still up to a million serfs bound to the soil in pre-Revolutionary France. There were also examples of new enserfment, as in Denmark, but in western Europe as a whole the milking-pail was used rather than the stick, the rack and the knout. And how that cow, the peasant, was milked by the state, the Church, the old lords and the new seigneurs, whose ingenuity in wringing out the last drops was almost illimitable.

What made the peasantry as a whole particularly vulnerable was the tenuous nature of their property rights. The seventeenth century falls into that lengthy transitional period, stretching from the twilight of the Middle Ages to the full dawning of the modern age, when the ancient concept of tenure in land had not been fully displaced by the later idea of property ownership. Under the manorial system, peasants in many parts of western Europe had been granted the right to cultivate a share of the arable land in the large open fields of the village and a customary right to use the surrounding commons and wastelands in return for work on the lord's demesne or the provision of other services. With the decay of the manorial system these services had gradually been commuted in most places for money rents, whose value had become derisory long before the seventeenth century owing to inflation and the debasement of currencies. Although the peasants retained their rights to use the land and could sell it or bequeath it or even lease it, usually for a limited period, they did not in most cases own it in the modern sense. In England, for example, conveyances of most peasants' land had to be made through the local manorial court, with the peasant surrendering his rights in the land to the lord, who then granted them out to the successor. Although the lord was in this sense superior to the peasant, he did not own the land either, for he could not disturb the peasant in his occupation of it, unless there was some breach of the customary obligations preserved either orally or in a written form in the manorial court rolls. The lord was something less than an owner and the peasant was something more than a tenant.

In the Middle Ages when land had seemed abundant and money had been scarce, superior lords could afford to grant out property rights freely to minor tenants, sometimes for quite frivolous services, such as those laid upon one tenant in Suffolk, England, 'to make a leap, a whistle and a fart *coram domino rege*'[13] on Christmas Day. But with the increase in population, which may have reached ninety or a hundred million in Europe by the middle of the seventeenth century, and the growth of a money economy, land could no longer be regarded as a laughing matter. John Locke, the prophet of the new age, was already preaching that 'the great and chief end of men uniting in commonwealths, and putting themselves under government, is the preservation of their property'[14] – not, significantly, the preservation of tenures or of customary rights. Hard cash was far more versatile than labour services. Where they could, many of the new lords, who

8 *Summer*, by Bruegel the Elder. A good harvest could bring contentment to both lord and peasant.

by the seventeenth century might be commoners, merchants, lawyers, or even in some cases former peasants, tried to squeeze their tenants out of their customary possession of the land, leasing it out to them again at rents which could be raised in line with increasing productivity or any depreciation in the currency; where that course was blocked, they tried to revive old feudal dues and territorial monopolies. In England, freemen, who owed their lord a distinct and specified service such as that mentioned above, had been protected in the tenure of their land by the royal courts since the twelfth century; but the majority of tenants were copyholders, who may have held between one-half and two-thirds of the land in England in the seventeenth century. These descendants of villeins, who had owed a certain number of days of unspecified labour to their lords, received

9 One of the most exhausting labour services was threshing. In this sixteenth-century illustration, peasants are seen at work in the central granary on a German estate.

little protection from the royal courts until the fifteenth or sixteenth centuries, and even then their causes continued to be decided mainly on the basis of local rules and customs appertaining to the manorial courts. Those who actually possessed a copy of the hereditary agreement to hold their land which was inscribed in the manorial court rolls were probably secure; but those who did not, or whose entry fine was not fixed, or whose lease had some other flaw in it, often became the victims of sharp-eyed lawyers or unscrupulous lords, who tried to force them to exchange their tenure for a short-term lease.

In France, royal courts may have gained authority somewhat later than in England, but they usually supported the principle of hereditary tenure which, as Marc Bloch has said, 'had become so firmly rooted by the sixteenth century that it could not be contested'.[15] But there are more ways than one of milking peasants. The value of the *cens* – an annual money rent – had become nominal by the seventeenth century, but feudal dues could be revived and local monopolies strengthened. The French peasant sometimes had to provide the lord with up to one-third of the annual produce of his land in addition to the *cens*, and usually had to pay him about 10 per cent of the purchase price if he sold his land. In most areas the peasant was also forced to use the lord's mill, oven and wine-press at the highest price the agent could extract, which invariably led to serious delays in the busy vintage and often to fraud of some kind. (It is little wonder that, with such noble-sponsored opportunities for peculation, the miller should have come down through history as the archetypal cheat and villain.) In addition, most western peasants had to pay tithes of up to one-tenth of the produce of the land, or a similar proportion in livestock, to monasteries, chapters, clergymen or lay owners, and with the increase in the power of the state a growing number of taxes were levied, of which the *taille* was the most important in France, plus other special impositions, often to make up the deficits produced by war, and indirect taxes on such necessities as salt.

It is virtually impossible to estimate which peasants in western Europe were the most severely crushed by these financial burdens, as their weight shifted from country to country, from region to region, and from year to year in response to the struggle among the members of the higher orders to secure a more comfortable position on the peasants' shoulders. But nowhere was the burden light. A fuller understanding of the vast range of taxes and tributes can be gained by glancing at the five-page appendix to Julius Klein's classic study of the *Mesta*, which gives a list of medieval and modern exactions in Spain. A few examples can serve as a general illustration for the whole of western Europe, for most of them were to be found in other countries at various times: *asadero*, a tax on villeins cultivating the commons with a spade; *cuevas*, a local tax on migrants living in caves; *fonsadero*, a war tax; *martiniega*, a tribute paid to lords on St Martin's Day; *nuncio*, the lord's right to take the best animal from a deceased vassal's estate; *mañería*, the king's or lord's share of an estate with no immediate heirs; *poyos*, a charge for using the village ovens; *recuage*, a royal tax for the upkeep of roads; *yerba*, a fee for cutting hay on the commons.[16] For many centuries the peasant was the main milch animal of western Europe.

The peasants also had to face an increasing challenge in their customary right to use the common land surrounding the village. The woods and wastelands, the marshes and the moors played an essential part in the non-waste peasant economy. They were a vast

21

10 Peasants' animals grazing on the wasteland rarely attained the well-fed luxuriance of these sheep being sheared on a prosperous farm in the late fifteenth century.

storehouse of natural treasures, the patrimony of the poor. From them the peasants obtained many of their necessities: rushes, which could be stripped, dried and soaked in fat to give a short-lived, spluttering artificial light; peat, which could be burnt as fuel, and whose salt-laden ash in the low-lying Netherlands was used for preserving herrings; bracken and moss for bedding, a favourite hiding-place for the cloth document-case containing the precious copyhold agreement; bark of trees, which could be plaited into cords; wax and honey; nuts and berries to supplement their often meagre diet; wild plants and herbs to be infused for tea or some medicinal purpose, and wood for making tools, furniture and footwear. The wastelands were also used for the grazing of such of their livestock – sheep, pigs and cattle – as could not be fed in the meadows, on the stubble of the harvested fields or on the weeds on the fallow. In addition, the woods had to satisfy the competing claims of ship-builder and house-builder, carpenter and charcoal-burner, until Abraham Darby's invention at the beginning of the eighteenth century of the coke-smelting process for making iron diminished some of the demands on English woodlands at least.

It is little wonder that, with the great demands made on them, these valuable natural resources should have been maltreated and squandered in many parts of Europe, particularly in the south, where the woodlands were ravaged by transhumant and sedentary sheep and by the cloven-hoofed goat, which will even climb into trees and shrubs in search of sustenance, leaving behind vast tracts of bleak erosion or unproductive *maquis*. (But who are we to condemn our ancestors when forest will regenerate in a few decades if the point of full-scale soil erosion has not been reached, whereas fossil fuels cannot be replaced in millions of years?)

If the ownership of the arable land was a mystery which was to tax the minds and line the pockets of medieval and modern lawyers for many centuries, the ownership of the commons was an even bigger enigma. In the seventeenth century they were still extensive in most countries, though the exact area is unknown: Gregory King, the social statistician, estimated that one-third of England and Wales consisted of forest, parks, commons, heaths, moors, mountain and barren land in 1688. (Forest, a legal rather than a botanical term, could include villages and pastures as well as commons and wasteland.) Some commons were shared by neighbouring villages; a few were legally held in common by members of the whole community; but probably the majority throughout western Europe were shared

23

11 In addition to his share of the common land, the lord also had his large estate which had been carved out of the wasteland by peasant labour.

jointly by lord and peasant, with the former usually reserving certain of the more valuable rights for himself. Of these, the most important and the most resented by the peasantry was the right of hunting – very rarely, in the seventeenth century, the fox, but far more commonly the wolf, the boar and that most prized of all quarries, the stag, which had for so many centuries provided such princely pleasure and highly organized spectator sport for monarchs and nobility.

The commons became one of the main areas where both the deprived and the unscrupulous could try to trace the pattern of their ambitions upon the soil. The very unattended desolation of so many commons, the sense of having been formed by no man's hand but only by God's, gave the squatter, the poacher, the landless some assurance of their natural rights, while the possibility of improving the soil doubtless eased the conscience of the encloser. Infringement of peasant rights did not go unchallenged: squatter's huts were

24

12 *Opposite* Frederick the Wise of Saxony hunting the stag: this noble prerogative was much resented by the peasants.

pulled down, fences demolished and intruding cattle driven off, and gallows were sometimes erected as a warning to the encloser. Throughout late medieval and modern times a long series of isolated skirmishes raged in the wastelands of western Europe. The usual justification for infringements was custom, which could be conveniently stretched to a date earlier than any written record; for example, it became part of the folklore of England that any squatter who succeeded in building some rude hut and lighting a fire in twenty-four hours had established his right to residence on the common.

The alignment of amorphous custom with the finer lineaments of the law was a laborious process extending over many centuries, with local might very often determining peasants' rights. By the middle of the seventeenth century, some commons had already been divided up by agreement between the lord and the peasants, with the former frequently retaining one-third for his personal use and selling out his dubious legal rights in the remainder to the peasantry. In some places, peasants' rights were abolished by superior force: the *intendant* in Dijon, France, noted in 1667 that 'all commons have been usurped and are either possessed by the lords of the communities or by persons in authority'.[17] There were, however, a few places, as in Seaford, Sussex, where rich men had renounced their rights in the commons to poorer peasants in Tudor times. And there were still many commons and wastelands in western Europe used communally by lord and peasant. The abolition of most common rights was a slow and gradual process, involving as it did not only a change in agricultural technology, but a much more profound transposition from an ancient way of life based on relatively small investments and enforced co-operation in the sharing of scarce resources to individual enterprise of the modern profit-seeking kind.

The feudal and manorial system did not extend evenly throughout the whole of western Europe. It had flourished in the Carolingian heartland between the Loire and the Rhine; it had been imposed on parts of England and Sicily and the south of Italy in that pincer-like movement of military conquest by the Normans in the eleventh century; and it had ended early in parts of northern Italy. Even within the central area, there had been many other forms of tenure. Sharecropping – what Karl Marx calls 'a form of transition . . . to capitalist rent'[18] – was common in late medieval times, particularly in the south of Europe, where a large initial investment was needed in tree crops; on the former demesnes of many lords; and in some of the newly colonized areas. Our knowledge of the history of *métayage*, in which landowner and tenant usually share the produce equally, is still limited, but it seems clear that where the lease was hereditary it could often be of benefit to both partners, protecting one against eviction and the other against inflation, which may partly account for the spread of the system in parts of France between the sixteenth and the eighteenth centuries. But too often in western Europe it seems to have degenerated into a competition between landlord and tenant to cheat each other of their rightful share. In Russia the *polovnik* (sharecropper) fared even worse, for he was among the first to be enserfed.

Within the manorial area there had always been some peasant freeholders, owing no obligations to a superior lord in the right to sell their land; there were probably even more outside this region, particularly, but not exclusively, in thinly populated areas with natural obstacles to agriculture in the form of hills, boulders or short growing seasons. Even in Scandinavia, long the home of relative freedom for the more prosperous peasants at least, many of the old-established odal freeholders had been turned into tenants by the middle of the seventeenth century. In Sweden, the need for support from the nobles in the Thirty Years War had forced the monarchy to grant or to sell many Crown estates to the nobility, who owned an estimated three-quarters of the kingdom by the end of the war in 1648. By that time it is thought that tenants outnumbered freeholders by three to one in Norway,[19] and in Denmark, where enserfment had started in the eastern islands in the fifteenth century, only about 6 per cent of the peasants retained their freeholds.[20]

Bowed down by these increasingly heavy burdens, the mass of peasants groaned and squirmed and sometimes stirred into open revolt. In England between 1649 and 1650 the Diggers, or True Levellers, made their unsuccessful attempts to take over some of the commons which they believed should rightfully be theirs. Throughout the seventeenth century many parts of France seethed with revolt, with major uprisings in Languedoc between 1629 and 1632, in Bordeaux in 1635, in Normandy in 1639, in Bordeaux again and in Brittany in 1675. There was an uprising in Switzerland in 1653 and one in Bohemia in 1679. In 1670 the general and prolonged discontent among the Russian serfs found a new leader in the Cossack Stenka Razin, who captured the town of Tsaritsyn on the Volga and then advanced north for eight hundred miles until he was defeated by the

13 A woodcut showing rebel peasants taking a knight prisoner in a German uprising.

tsar's armies. All of these uprisings were crushed, some with barbaric inhumanity as in Russia, where the troops took a dreadful revenge upon the rebels, burning villages, executing thousands and impaling others who 'howled for three days on the stakes on which they were thrust'.[21] Most of these revolts formed parts of wider uprisings, as peasant rebellions have always tended to do. Their immediate causes were various – land tenure, falling cereal prices, increased taxes – but the deeper cause was everywhere the same, a despairing protest at the intolerable burden of their fate.

With few exceptions, the peasants have always been defeated in their revolts. Isolated in their small communities, badly organized, ill equipped, and divided to a certain extent among themselves by family and by wealth, they were easy to crush, village by village, region by region. Throughout history the peasant, who was so often bent over some back-breaking task with the sickle or the flail, was the inferior of the mounted man, whose physical ascendancy gave him his power and seeming superiority. Both literally and metaphorically the peasant had to look up to his lord and master. His avenues of escape were few and usually unwelcome – into some menial task in the town or into an even more dangerous or onerous occupation as a mercenary or a common seaman. The peasant wanted security to cultivate the soil in the place where he had been born; but this seemingly simple aim was always most difficult to fulfil.

It would be false to exaggerate the extent either of peasant revolts or of landowners' oppression. There is obviously a human tendency for more to be heard of bad times and of bad landowners than of good. In many places there must have been long periods when the cyclic rhythm of harvest and fallow was undisturbed by any major shifts in the relationships between peasants and their lords, and the village seemed to be wrapped in a sleeping solemnity. As André J. Bourde has observed of France: 'In the rural society before 1750 the seigneurs were often not too exacting. Most of the *petite noblesse* still lived on its estates in a spirit of severe thrift.'[22] But below the quiet surface there was an implicit social tension, not only between peasant and lord, but also between rich and poor peasants. The peasant world was so circumscribed by social regulation that very few could escape from it. They were imprisoned by the structure of society so that like starving rats in a wire cage they could only feed on each other. The forces of money and the market economy which caused high society to press down so relentlessly operated no less strongly within the village world. This combined with the random operation of natural factors – the chance visitations of death, illness, plague and famine – to produce great disturbances within these small communities.

14 A detail of reapers from the Luttrell Psalter (c. 1340) illustrating how the peasant, bent over his task, had literally as well as metaphorically to look up to the lord.

The history of the social structure of the European countryside is a relatively new study, but it is already clear that the old village world, which we were once accustomed to think of as in some way static, placid and simple, was economically and socially highly complex and changeable. The village was a closely interwoven web of financial obligations, a ceaseless clearing-house of debts not only to the state and to lords, but also to richer peasants and to tradesmen in the towns. Even a cursory glance at some seventeenth-century inventories will show the extent of this indebtedness: the peak of credit was reached in the spring after the difficulties of the winter, falling off considerably in autumn after a successful harvest. Richer peasants were one of the main sources of credit: when Cornelius Humphrey, a substantial yeoman of Sussex, England, died in 1697 he was owed £426 in 'desperate debts' and an unstated amount in good debts. In these closely-knit communities, where so many persons might be inter-related, the fortunes of families were of no less importance than individuals. There were feuds, familial obligations and possibly no fewer marriages of convenience than in high society, with younger peasant sons marrying older widows to inherit their land, and then taking a younger bride after their first wife's death. The buying and selling of land among the free peasants, which is recorded in England from the twelfth century, had resulted in a few slow climbs to individual affluence and an even greater number of falls.

By the middle of the seventeenth century, a small number of peasants in western Europe had become as rich as some of the minor gentry and the smaller merchants: the yeomen of England, the *fermiers-receveurs* of France, the surviving odal freeholders of Scandinavia. They had risen to the brink of social acceptance, so that the English yeoman and his wife might occasionally be dignified by a title – Goodman and Goodwife or Goody.[23] Some of their descendants would be able to rise by way of trade, finance and the law to the ranks of gentry or its equivalent; this could happen over three or four generations in France, while in England some exceptional sons, like Bishop Latimer in the sixteenth century, had already made the transition in their own lifetime. On the whole, as Slicher van Bath has pointed out, it was probably easier for a peasant to rise in arable farming than it was in livestock farming, which needed larger amounts of capital, and easier in periods of agricultural depression than in booms when land was more difficult to obtain.[24] But for the few who rose, there were a far greater number who could fall below the level of sufficiency: among them were the cottager of England, the *manouvrier* of France, the *Kötter* of north-west Germany and the *Seldner* of southern Germany. At an even lower level there was an ever-shifting, ever-changing mass of unemployed and unemployable – the paupers, the squatters, the sick, the beggars, the vagrants, the bandits – who may have accounted for as much as 15 per cent of the population in times of depression and even more in times of war, but who in more normal periods possibly totalled 5 to 10 per cent of the population.[25]

The peasant world of the seventeenth century is a fascinating study. Agrarian and social historians have refined new techniques of local history which allow us, as it were, to lift the cobweb-covered dustcap off some microscope to peer down at the bustle of activity in the village below. The pioneer study by W. G. Hoskins[26] of the village of Wigston in Leicestershire has become a classic of its kind. We can watch the inhabitants, mainly 'middling and small peasant landowners, farming the three open fields that still lay unimpaired all around';[27] see how the number of households had doubled over the past century to 140 or so by 1625, creating pressure on the building land; and observe the growth of a class of able-bodied poor who, by 1670, accounted for about one-sixth of the population. The author follows the mixed fortunes of various families, some like the Pawleys and the Smiths who had risen from the ranks of substantial yeomen in 1524 and were 'either recognised "gentry" or about to become so'[28] by 1670, and others, like the Chamberlains and the Astills, who had either left the village or declined from yeomen into small peasant farmers or poor labourers.

We can cross the Channel to explore with Pierre Goubert[29] the region of Beauvaisis in northern France during the last quarter of the seventeenth century. There we can observe the struggle of the *manouvriers* in the northern parts to keep their families by growing maslin (a mixture of wheat and rye), beans, cabbages and hemp on their few acres of ground, and their attempts to escape from their perpetual tangle of debts by working for richer peasants 'at trivial, seasonal and occasional jobs'.[30] In the softer countryside to the south the *manouvriers* were somewhat better off, as more of them were able to keep a cow on the rolling pastures; there were also a number of more prosperous peasants, the *airiers* or market-gardeners, growing asparagus and artichokes for the Paris markets near by, and vine-growers who also made fans, lace and fancy wear for the inhabitants of the capital. In the whole of the region there were some, though not many, really prosperous peasants, the *laboureurs*, who owned their own plough and horses and farmed up to seventy-five acres or so; 'at the apex of the peasant hierarchy'[31] were the *fermiers-receveurs*, who leased large farms of up to 250 acres of arable land, usually from some monastery or abbey, and collected the seignorial dues and tithes from other peasants. We can observe in detail the financial and farming transactions of one *fermier*, Claude Dumesnil of Goincourt, with his twelve horses, two ploughmen and two carters, 160 pigeons and two dozen turkeys, his hundred barrels of wine and cider and his own small library of religious and travel books. We can travel further south in France with Le Roy Ladurie[32] to watch the graziers, dairymen and transhumant shepherds at work in High Languedoc, and the peasants of Low Languedoc growing a whole range of exotic vegetables and fruits – aubergines, peppers, maize and melons – to meet the limited demands of the towns.

Superficially, some of these peasants may appear to be not entirely unlike us in their rises to economic prosperity and their falls, their ambitions to succeed and their failures, their desire to gain a sufficiency of wealth or an abundance. Yet in reality most of them were very different, not only in the more obvious circumstances of their lives – their homes, food, work and clothes – but also in their basic attitudes and customs and, in the broadest anthropological sense, their culture, of which a few small fragments have come down to us today in the form of folk-tales, 'superstitions', and craft objects preserved in museums. All these are now bereft of the significance they possessed then, when modern forces had only shaken the foundations of the distinctive peasant world and not destroyed its inner substance.

Material shortages there may have been, but this only helped to increase the significance of all objects within the immediate environment, just as the loss of one sense may help to stimulate the sensitivity of others. It also emphasized the importance of accumulation. The countryside conserved the skills, the values and the attitudes of the past. Techniques of making objects for daily use, and their design, were handed down by example from father to son and from mother to daughter in each village, possibly in some cases from early medieval times when their ancestors had been forced to work in manorial workshops as part of their labour services to their lord, or even from some more distant era. Their celebrations also had connections with the past. The great events in personal and agrarian life – birth, marriage,

15 In an otherwise austere life, creativity and love of beauty found their outlet in the production of pieces like this Norwegian tapestry of the wise virgins – a common theme in folk art.

death, the beginning of winter, the resumption of ploughing, the gathering of the harvest – were celebrated with fire festivals, magic rites and incantations, dance and song, which may in some cases have originated in prehistoric times. E. Estyn Evans, for example, mentions 'the survival of a pre-instrumental pentatonic scale in the haunting folk tunes of north-western Europe, from Ireland to Finland'.[33] These songs and tales, proverbs and riddles were handed down from one generation to another, preserving the collective attitudes of the past, where myth and history, hopes and actualities all meet and mingle. In the same way, religious attitudes from earlier times were preserved, so that the Christian cross and icon did not seem out of place in what was also, or once had been, an animistic grove. Peasant culture was utilitarian and eclectic.

The peasant's hopes and visions were bounded by the fields or forests, the moors or mountains surrounding him, where he acted out his brief and sometimes unavailing struggle to wrest a meagre living from the unforgiving soil. 'His hand guides the plough and the plough his thoughts,' wrote John Earle in 1628, 'and his ditch

33

16, 17 Country customs, concentrating on constant aspects of the rural calendar such as the renewal of life in the spring, remained unchanged for centuries. Compare Bruegel's *May Dance* of 1634 (*above*) with Breton's nineteenth-century French treatment of a similar theme in *La Saint-Jean* (*opposite*). In the eclectic tradition of peasant culture, pagan celebrations were held near the Christian churches visible in the background.

and landmark is the very mound of his meditations.'[34] It was this limitation of vision which gave the peasant world an integration such as modern man has never known. The home was not separate from work; work was not separate from celebration; celebration was not separate from the home. In Norway, long a stronghold of *bondekultur* (peasant culture), 'a considerable proportion of the oldest farms were centres of a formal religious worship, in which the landholder figured as high priest'.[35] Writing had scarcely penetrated the peasant world to separate learning from activity, myth from history, individual art from collective expression, so that each person carried his own share of the cultural tradition. In Finland alone, the folk-poetry that has been recorded runs to over a million verses.[36] It was transmitted to new generations by word of mouth, often in local dialects and traditional languages – Old Norse in Norway, Flemish in northern Belgium – cutting off the peasants even more decisively from the foreign-speaking rulers in the towns.

It was this isolation which allowed the past to grow such deep roots in each locality, making each hamlet, each village, a living world in microcosm with its own separate customs and traditions. Peasant culture was manifested inevitably at the parochial level, but both in content and in method it had a truly surprising universality, indicating perhaps the ancient diffusion of some common culture, similar but separate reactions to an ubiquitous fate, or more mobility and contacts in the peasant world of the past than we have been led to believe. From Ireland in the west to Russia in the east, from Italy in the south to Finland in the north, there is a great uniformity in the folk-tales and songs with their common themes of magic objects or supernatural tasks and helpers and their jokes and anecdotes about parsons and priests, crafty millers, married couples, nagging wives who are even worse than the devil, lucky accidents and 'horrid money'.[37] They shared a simple delight in the common festivals of celebration and the ordinary pleasures of daily life, as in this wooing song from Kent, England, first printed in 1611:

> *Ich will put on my best white sloppe*
> *And ich will weare my yellow hose;*
> *And on my head a good gray hat,*
> *And in't Ich sticke a lovely rose.*[38]

Such were the simple dreams of simple folk.

18 Peter Paul Rubens, *Landscape with a Rainbow*: a seventeenth-century landscape showing mixed farming, arable and dairy, in Belgium.

II CHANGES IN AGRICULTURE

By the middle of the seventeenth century there was already a considerable diversity in European agriculture. The most primitive form of cultivation, the slash-and-burn method, which was almost certainly used by peasant pioneers to make the original forest clearings in prehistoric times, was still in common use in many countries, in areas ranging from the hillsides of Sicily to the dense forests of Scandinavia and the huge forested plains of Poland and Russia between the tundra zone to the north and the steppes to the south. The trees were burnt and the ash, rich in potash, was scattered over the soft moist soil. The ground was tilled for a few years before the cultivators moved on to another site, returning after a lapse of twenty-five years or more when bushes and trees had grown again. Other peasants used the infield-outfield system. A small clearance was cultivated continuously, being kept fertile by means of manure and humus collected from the surrounding wasteland, which was used mainly as grazing land for the community's livestock, though parts of it were probably brought into temporary cultivation from time to time. In north-west, central and eastern Europe there were much larger areas of open-field cultivation, in which the large fields, divided into strips, probably as a result of increase in population, were usually cultivated in common. In the south of Europe, and in some other places, there were square-shaped open fields. And almost everywhere there were enclosed fields, particularly in the livestock areas, some of which were of considerable antiquity.

There was also a surprising degree of specialization: Eric Kerridge recognizes no less than forty-one clearly defined farming areas – or 'countries'[1] as he prefers to call them – in England alone by 1560, ranging from Chalk to Cheshire Cheese and from the Western Waterlands to the Wealden Vales. Similar areas of specialization had also developed in other European countries as a result of countless trials and experiments by largely unremembered peasants, lords and farmers. Agriculture is affected by many different factors, including

19 The slash–and–burn method of land clearance in use in Scandinavia in the late nineteenth century.

the structure of society as a whole, the changing social, economic and demographic pressures of the age, and the nature of the local environment. As a result of the complex interaction of these factors there was little uniformity in agricultural progress in individual countries, and even less in Europe as a whole, but only a slow accumulation of change over many years, or even centuries, with numerous regional variations and sometimes great reversals. 'The improvement of the ground', wrote Francis Bacon, 'is the most natural obtaining of riches; for it is our great mother's blessing, the earth's; but it is slow.'[2] The old farming world, which we were once accustomed to think of as in some way uniform and static, was in fact highly localized and in a process of slow, but continual, ebb and flow. That is what makes it particularly unsafe to generalize about agricultural history: there are almost always disturbing exceptions. Slash-and-burn methods, for example, persisted in parts of Russia into the present century, and the last forest clearings were made in northern Sweden as late as 1950.

Nevertheless, taking Europe as a whole there were, in very general terms, some broad distinctions between the kinds of farming practised in southern, central and northern Europe, caused mainly by natural factors, of which mean temperature, altitude, rainfall and the nature

38

of the terrain were the most important. Although they operated with great variability in each locality, they did provide different challenges and opportunities and set some limitations to what could successfully be grown in each of these vast geographical regions, so that the northern limit of the Mediterranean region is marked to this day by olive groves. Progress in agriculture, and therefore to a great extent the development of society as a whole in the pre-industrial age, rested very largely on the success of peasants, farmers and landowners in responding to these opportunities, in evolving techniques appropriate to their environment and searching for major innovations, and on their willingness and ability to adopt these. Their choices were often tentative and fumbling, being based on instinct, luck, or greed rather than rational decision; but, in aggregate, they did have profound effects on the whole of society, not only in the fundamental aspects of the general creation of economic wealth, and of providing a sufficiency of food for the total population, including the agriculturally much less productive inhabitants of the towns, but also in the finest details, such as the common daily diet and rural transport. The importance of agriculture in the seventeenth century cannot be exaggerated; it still shaped the daily lives, many of the attitudes and much of the culture of the vast majority of the European population, determined their main opportunities for employment and, above all, to a considerable extent, their chances of survival, the continuance of life or the imminence of death.

The sunlit, Janus-faced lands of the south, with their huge mountain ranges – the Pyrenees, the Alps, the Apennines and the Caucasus – descending through foothills or elevated plateaux to flood-prone plains or marshlands, have always produced what J. M. Houston has called 'a tantalising paradox of fruitfulness and frugality'.[3] The southern lands experienced their main agricultural revolution very early in the areas which were favoured by more abundant rainfall or which could be irrigated, the 'experimental greenhouse'[4] of the western world, where exotic fruits like the cherry and the lemon were already being grown in classical times and where a large range of new crops, including the peach, the pomegranate, the orange, the apricot, rice, sugar-cane and saffron, were introduced by the Arabs who occupied much of Spain and Portugal for nearly five hundred years.[5] (The European debt to the Middle East is very great: the cultivation of wheat and barley and the domestication of sheep, goats, asses and, possibly, pigs and cattle, started there in Neolithic times.)

The irrigated fringes of the Mediterranean world had a lush appearance which was deceptive, for much of the region was inimical to agriculture. The searing summer heat and the annual drought inhibited agricultural activity in the south. The need to conserve the moisture in the subsoil suggested the system of dry farming, in which the field was ploughed and cross-ploughed with a light scratch plough to keep the surface free of weeds. Although the connection between types of plough and the shape of fields is still a matter for debate,[6] this may have accounted in part for the prevalence of the square-shaped (or irregular) open fields which were a characteristic feature of so many parts of the south, and, perhaps more certainly, made it somewhat easier for the peasant to own his own plough team, since only two oxen were needed as against the six or eight which had to be used to pull the heavy wheeled plough in the north-west of Europe. Harvesting, too, presented fewer problems, as there was much less likelihood of the crop being spoiled by sudden rains, and the grain could be threshed beneath the hooves of oxen or mules in the open air instead of being stored in a barn and threshed with a flail as in north-west Europe. But the shortness of the growing season made the sowing of a spring crop of oats or other grain generally uncertain. As a consequence, much of the south remained yoked to the ancient two-course crop rotation, in which half the land was left fallow every year. Lynn White Jr[7] argues that, as a result, insufficient fodder was produced to feed working farm horses, so that the slower-moving ox, which can be fed on hay and grass, remained the main draught animal, giving the south its slow and seemingly indolent air. The classic crops in the south remained the long-established trinity of winter-sown wheat, and the olive and the vine, whose long roots could reach deep down for moisture below the parched surface of the midsummer soil. It was these crops which produced the basic ingredients of the southern diet, unchanged to this day: bread or pasta, wine and olive oil.

The nature of the terrain in the south also had important consequences for agriculture. From antiquity, the vast mountainous regions had encouraged the practice of transhumance – the annual migration of flocks of sheep and goats between the rough grazings in the uplands and the marshes and valleys below. Although transhumance occurred elsewhere in Europe, it was most common in the Mediterranean region and was developed to the greatest extent in Spain, where the *Mesta,* a privileged association of shepherds, was

20 Spanish sheep in a fold outside the town of Ecija in Andalusia: a sixteenth-century engraving.

granted a royal charter in 1273. The sheep were bred for wool, not for meat: as Julius Klein has remarked, the long annual journeys of between 150 and 450 miles each way made the flesh too tough to eat, and in that anti-Semitic society a preference for pork, rather than mutton, acted as an assurance of good faith.[8] Every year, about the middle of September, the flocks of merino sheep, which by 1526 had reached the phenomenal total of three and a half million, set out from the mountainous areas of León and Logroño in Old Castile for the range lands on the plateau of Estremadura and in the valley of the Guadalquivir, and from the heights round Cuenca in New Castile for the lowlands of Murcia. They made the return journey every April, travelling fifteen miles or so a day along the *cañadas*, or sheep-walks, reserved for them. Their white, kinky fleeces, smeared with red clay or ochre as a protective device or a distinguishing mark, were so highly valued elsewhere that they became one of Spain's most profitable exports to Flanders, England and Italy. Exports of the sheep themselves were forbidden, and it was not until the eighteenth century that other European countries managed to establish flocks of their own.

These migratory movements were at first strictly controlled, but the sheep were later given their head, particularly after Ferdinand and Isabella came to the Spanish throne in 1479. The gradual widening of the *cañadas*, the depredation of commons by shepherds who were allowed to cut branches to build their cabins and to burn trees to create improved pastures, the nibbling of young shoots by the millions of sheep themselves, all combined to destroy the natural cover and to allow the hostile rocks to swell like grey blisters through the thin, eroded soil. The Spanish authorities were well aware of the evil effects of this excessive pastoralism, as their feebly enforced forest conservation decrees of 1518, 1548 and 1567 show, but they needed the easily enforceable taxes on the *Mesta* to finance their innumerable wars and their exploitation of the New World. Not for the first time in Europe, or the last, the peasants' stint of grazing land and the people's need for bread were sacrificed to quick profits and the greed of nobles, ecclesiastical and military orders and the smaller shepherds, so that grain had increasingly to be imported from foreign countries. By the middle of the seventeenth century the *Mesta* had already passed its peak, even though its flocks still totalled about two millions, but it had set a pattern of exploitation and bad husbandry which proved to be enduring, so that even now some of the unimproved regions of Spain remain unparalleled for their eroded desolation anywhere in the world, 'even in the western U.S.A. or Algeria'.[9] In 1600 the central areas of Castile probably still contained almost one-third of the total Spanish population (about twice as much as now); but, with the decline of the *Mesta*, farmers started to turn their land over to sedentary sheep-raising, which reduced the demand for labour. This led to depopulation of the countryside. Whole villages became deserted and hordes of beggars thronged the roads, producing the same familiar tale of woe wherever agriculture had been sacrificed to pastoralism. It had occurred also in England where, as Sir Thomas More complained in 1516, the sheep had been allowed to 'eat up and swallow down the very men themselves',[10] though probably the main effects of depopulation, which may have started in about 1440, had almost reached their end when he was writing his words.[11]

North-west Europe shared some of the problems of the south, but the natural challenges and opportunities were on the whole very different. In that more temperate region of frequent heavy skies, mists and rain, less immediately enticing than the Mediterranean area, a more productive agriculture could flourish because, as A. N. Duckham has pointed out, 'it has soils which, though often acid, can be fairly easily improved; secondly, a climate which has a greater margin of agricultural safety; and thirdly, a growing season that is longer than in many other natural regions'.[12] The summer rainfall made it possible for a crop of oats or barley to be sown in the spring, producing a three-course rotation of winter wheat, spring grain (or, from about the tenth century, a leguminous crop, such as peas or beans), followed by a year of fallow. The more generally productive three-course rotation was introduced into north-west Europe in the eighth century or even earlier, presumably to feed a growing population. It also provided sufficient surplus for working farm horses. By the twelfth century at the latest, Lynn White Jr has calculated, it could increase productivity by one-half and the amount of land that could be cultivated by one-eighth compared with the two-course rotation.[13] The larger grain production and the links between arable farming and livestock, generally closer than those in the south, helped to give the north-west of Europe its characteristic diet of bread, ale (or cider in apple-growing regions) and animal fat instead of oil. In central and eastern Europe, with their colder winters, rye, which is more frost-resistant, was frequently grown instead of wheat, while barley and oats were common everywhere.

The heavier rainfall in north-west Europe made it necessary to use a different kind of plough in the lowlands to ridge and furrow the soil so that excess water would drain away. A heavy wheeled plough was generally used, though not exclusively, with a coulter and a share to cut the soil and a fixed mouldboard to stack the furrows side by side. The use of this plough may have been partly responsible for the characteristic strip pattern of the open fields (though that theory is now much disputed, and many other factors were almost certainly involved); the need to employ a team of six or eight oxen made it more difficult than it was in the south for the peasant to own his own plough team, producing a tendency for more co-operation, at a price, in the ploughing of fields. The summer rainfall also made harvesting more uncertain than it was in the south.

Further north again, in many parts of Scandinavia, there were different problems, as the harder winters made it unprofitable or impossible to sow a grain crop in the autumn. In the extreme north, agriculture itself could make no impact on the snowy wastes where the Lapps led a nomadic life, as a few thousand of them still do even now. Every year they migrated with their herds of reindeer from the lichen pastures in the mountains to the peat-bogs of the elevated plateaux and the coasts, sleeping side by side under a communal cover in their tents of reindeer skins, washing in the snow, eating reindeer steaks, infusing drinks from plants and berries, drinking reindeer milk on ordinary occasions and fermenting it for their celebrations.

Within these vast geographical regions, there were smaller areas where natural factors combined in a particular way to suggest special possibilities. In Britain, for example, the hilly regions of the north and the west had a moister, wetter climate than the south and east, providing luxuriant pastures in some places and barren land suitable for little but rough grazings or forestry in others. As a result the former areas had been for many centuries the traditional centres for livestock farming, which, in its turn, tended to produce a particular kind of rural society, more rigidly stratified than in the south and east of England, with fewer intermediate groups between the richer family farmers who could afford the heavy investment in livestock farming, and the living-in farm servants and specialist workers who were hired by the year at annual fairs. The smaller labour force needed for livestock farming produced a lower density of population which, before the increasing dispersal of upland farms in the eighteenth century, tended to live in small hamlets containing several farm-steads – very different from the nucleated villages of the Midlands and the south. As far as we know their daily diet tended to be different too, with a much greater emphasis on meat, cheese, curds and whey. Writing in 1776, Adam Smith said: 'It is not more than a century ago that in many parts of the highlands of Scotland, butcher's-meat was as cheap or cheaper than even bread made of oat-meal.'[14]

Natural factors operate with such variability, making it possible, for example, to grow crops on the south-facing slopes of Alpine valleys but only trees on the other side, that even without any secular changes in agricultural demand or any pressures from high society, there would still have been considerable local variations in farming.

Were long-term changes in the climate of Europe one of the crucial factors in agricultural development? On an extended time-scale, they obviously were, for it was the final retreat of the ice, from about 8000 BC, which allowed southern trees to spread northwards and the mammoth and the reindeer to be replaced by the wild pig and the deer of the Upper Palaeolithic age. But did much smaller changes of only one or two degrees in the mean temperature of Europe occur over much more limited periods of one or two hundred years, and, if they did, what effects did they have on agriculture? The study of historical climatology is still not sufficiently advanced for any pronouncements to be made with certainty, but it is worth bearing in mind that a change of only two degrees Fahrenheit in mean temperature is the equivalent of a difference in altitude of some

540 feet, so that a rise in mean temperature might have been sufficient to turn some rough grazings into cultivable land, if other natural factors were favourable. On the other hand, as Le Roy Ladurie[15] has observed, any climatic changes of this kind, if they did occur, would have had variable effects throughout Europe, as dryness is the great problem of the south, high humidity that of the north-west, and coldness that of the north.

Challenges are just as important as opportunities in farming. Some of the most advanced and intensive forms of agriculture were to be found in areas which were but slightly blessed with natural advantages. In agriculture, one of the main keys to progress is the control of water supplies – the irrigation of semi-arid lands and the draining of flood-prone marshlands and coastal regions. For these improvements the south leaned more heavily on its past than did north-west Europe: its long and varied history of Roman domination and foreign occupation was more firmly imprinted on the soil. The evidence of these ancient endeavours is still to be found to this day on many southern hillsides, terraced to retain moisture and to prevent soil erosion. In these small plots the vine has flourished for centuries by the dry-stone wall or bank of earth, while wheat and vegetables for the family and vetches for the donkey or the mule have been inter-calated between the olive and the fruit trees. The past is apparent, too, in the *huertas* of eastern Spain, with their *noria* or water-wheels driven by donkeys or mules, and the elaborate irrigation system of canals controlled in Valencia by the Tribunal of Waters which still meets weekly outside the cathedral, built on the site of a former Arab mosque. In the Po valley, on the borderline between northern and southern Europe, the Italian communes had started the slow process of improvement, which continued almost unchecked from medieval times to the present century, transforming the lake-strewn marsh-lands into the most advanced agricultural region of Italy. In the twelfth century the first great irrigation work, the *Naviglio Grande*, was completed. The floating of water-meadows, in which a stream or river was artificially diverted to flow over pastures to fertilize them and to provide a richer and earlier crop of grass, was introduced. In the fourteenth and fifteenth centuries, rice started to be cultivated widely on the Lombardy plain, and the mulberry tree was planted on the hillsides for the breeding of the silkworm.

Improvements further north were to be even more influential, both directly and indirectly, for the future course of agriculture in

45

many parts of Europe, and, through that, for the development of society as a whole. The Low Countries in particular had very few natural endowments as far as agriculture was concerned. The confluence of three great European rivers, the Rhine, the Meuse and the Scheldt, produced a huge swampy delta region of large and small islands, lakes and shifting dunes of sand shaken ceaselessly into new patterns by the action of wind, tides and waves. Behind the littoral there was another large area of low-lying peaty swampland and sandy heath, much of which lay open to the encroaching of the sea wherever the fragile barrier of sand-dunes along the coast was breached. Over the course of centuries, through the ceaseless work of countless millions of forgotten individuals, the region was to be transformed into one of the most advanced farming areas in Europe. The process began in the extreme north more than two thousand years ago when the Frisians started to build huge mounds, called *terpen*, up to forty acres in extent and rising thirty feet above sea-level, as sites for their villages in the marshlands which were flooded twice a day. They also constructed smaller mounds, *wieren*, which were uninhabited, but used as refuges for cattle stranded by the daily floods. At least a thousand *terpen* were built in Friesland and the neighbouring province of Groningen, initially, it is believed, by scooping up the peaty mud with bare hands and carrying it to the site in baskets and later on sleds.[16] In the eighth century at the latest, the Frisians started flood-prevention works by joining groups of *terpen* together with a dike or high embankment and ditch, and later set themselves the even more ambitious task of constructing a sea-wall round the whole of Friesland.

Similar works of coastal protection were started on a large scale further south by the counts of Flanders in the eleventh century, and possibly somewhat later in the province of Holland in the Netherlands. Earth embankments were built, canal and irrigation channels were dug, and rivers were dredged by means of a large scoop dragged towards a floating wooden platform by a capstan, the work being supervised by dike-masters in their tall pointed hats, loose jerkins and baggy trousers and greased leather thigh-length boots. The much greater energy input provided by the windmill allowed more lakes to be drained to form fertile polders, though Jan Leeghwater's seventeenth-century scheme to drain the forty-thousand-acre Haarlem lake by using 160 windmills was not put into effect until the middle of the nineteenth century when steam-driven pumps were used.

21, 22 *Above* A sketch by Roelandt Savery, dated *c.* 1610, of a 'mud mill' similar to those used to dredge the waterways in the Netherlands. *Below The Water Mill*, by Meindert Hobbema (1638–1709): falling water is one of the oldest technological sources of power in the countryside.

23 A varied group of Dutch windmills from a sixteenth-century engraving.

The first certain record of a windmill in western Europe was at Weedley, Yorkshire, in 1185.[17] Windmills replaced the earlier water-mills not only for grinding grain but also for an immense variety of industrial functions; they were specially adapted in the Low Countries for works of land reclamation by fitting a scoop wheel, later replaced by a screw pump which could lift water three times as high, up to sixteen feet. By using a group of mills in series, excess water could be lifted out of lakes and canals and pumped into ring canals round the polders, where it could find an outlet to the sea. Windmills were an ideal source of power in the Low Countries, where the winds blow free and uninterrupted, and the flat country-side also allowed them to be used as primitive semaphore stations, to send working instructions by altering the position of the sails and personal messages of celebration by decorating the sails at times of births and marriages.

By the middle of the seventeenth century some parts of the Low Countries had already been given their artificial, geometric appearance, characteristic of the region to this day, of neat, quadrilateral polders intersected by canals and supervised by attendant windmills.

24, 25 *Above* By the mid-seventeenth century, some of the Dutch country-side in the west had been drained to form a pattern of quadrilateral fields surrounded by ditches and canals. *Below* A Dutch flax-bleaching field: land improvement and intensive forms of agriculture made possible the growing of commercial crops.

26 Paulus Potter's painting of *The Young Bull* dates from 1647. Selective cattle-breeding, however, was practised in parts of the Low Countries from the late Middle Ages, and influenced the later agricultural revolution in England.

It was in this area, from the late Middle Ages, that intensive forms of agriculture were developed which were to astonish foreign visitors, particularly the English, so greatly. The region became justly famed for its cattle-breeding, its horticulture and its commercial crops, such as flax, madder and hops, which were often grown on quite small patches of formerly poor sandy soil by intensive means – deep digging, heavy manuring and constant weeding. Many of the agricultural innovations which, in aggregate, were to be designated as revolutionary in eighteenth-century England, had been introduced many years before in the Low Countries, even though they were sometimes used for different purposes and on a smaller scale. Among the most important were the use of beds and rows for sowing seed, instead of broadcasting it; the light wheeled plough of Gelderland and Flanders, with its single handle, which could be drawn by a pair of horses; convertible husbandry, in which the land was sown with crops and then put down to grass or clover for four or five years for use as pasture to rest and fertilize it; and the sowing of fodder crops such as lucerne and turnips in the fallow year, to break the vicious circle of the three-course crop rotation.

The replacement of the fallow year by a fodder crop or a ley greatly increased the number of livestock which could be kept and the yield of crops. Formerly, the land had to be rested for a year after it had borne two exhausting grain crops; but the cultivation of a crop like turnips, which require frequent weeding, kept the land in good condition and provided valuable fodder to feed a larger number of animals, which then produced more manure for use on the arable land. Previously, some animals had to be slaughtered every autumn, and those that were kept were often so weakened through lack of food that by the spring they had to be dragged out to the fields by their tails – the German *Schwanzvieh* – though agrarian historians now tend to discount the tales of massive animal slaughters every autumn.[18] To provide even more manure, sheep in some parts of the Low Countries were folded indoors on sanded floors at night so that, as one English visitor observed in 1650, they could 'tread their Dung and Piss into the sand'[19] which was then carted out to manure the fields. Even these innovations did not provide sufficient fertilizer for the most intensive farmers, who had to rely on supplementary supplies such as wood ash, or night soil transported from the towns along canals, rivers and roads to their farms. Before the age of artificial fertilizers, farmers and peasants had to seek ceaselessly for new sources of manure in seaweed, human sewage, peat ash, town garbage, pigeon dung, crushed shells and bones, soot, brine, ox blood, industrial refuse from tanners and furriers and later, in the middle of the nineteenth century, guano – the dried excrement of sea birds imported in great quantities into England, particularly from islands off Peru. These activities doubtless contributed towards the earthy, mucky image of the peasant even in the less salubrious ages of the past.

Why did improved methods of agriculture develop first in these areas? It would appear that they were a response to a combination of different challenges and opportunities – the natural difficulties of the local environment, the increase in the density of the population, and above all the growth in the size and number of cities and towns in the Low Countries. As the focal point of international trade shifted north from the Mediterranean, it came to concentrate more and more on these small countries so favourably situated at the geographical crossroads of Europe, with sea-routes leading to the Baltic and the Iberian peninsula and across the North Sea to England, and southward, routes along the great rivers, which had inherently provided so many

51

obstacles to agriculture. Cities developed first in the southern part of the Low Countries, and later further north: before the middle of the seventeenth century it is estimated that over half the population of the province of Holland was living in towns.

These large urban communities of prosperous merchants had multiple effects on the countryside. They provided the necessary capital for investment in agriculture, and a regular and profitable demand for farm produce, not only for food but also for industrial crops for the primary industry of textiles. Once man has attended to the needs of his belly he concentrates on clothing his back. Textiles, which were once so closely associated with agriculture, have had an enormous impact on society. To realize all that is involved, one has only to consider all the intricate processes and the diverse skills which contribute towards the manufacture of even an unadorned gown, such as that favoured in the northern parts of the Low Countries in the sixteenth century, compared with the simple operation of shearing a sheep for its fleece in the days when only skins or hides were worn. Flax (which requires no less than five separate processes in its preparation), hemp, cotton and wool had to be produced or imported; woad, madder and weld had to be grown for dyes; peasants' wives had to be employed in spinning. The Low Countries also had some direct impact on farming in other countries through their demands for wool from England, Germany and Spain, for brandy from France, grain from eastern Europe and cattle from Denmark. Similar factors account for the improvements in agriculture in the Po valley, though the industrial base in Milan was more diversified. The influence of large cities was predominant in many other areas of agricultural improvement – in parts of Beauvaisis, for example, and in some of the counties round London.

What part did the peasantry play in these improvements? Were they simply backward, inefficient smallholders and petty farmers who stubbornly tried to halt the march of agricultural progress, as we have so often been led to believe? It appears to be increasingly difficult to sustain such a generalized view, for it is now clear that many of them played a major part in improving the land and possibly, though this is much less certain, in introducing some of the innovations where they had the opportunity to do so. The careful soil conservation practised in the peasant republic of Friesland, which successfully defended itself against an attempt at domination by foreign princes in the thirteenth century, may usefully be contrasted with the stupidity of monarchs in Castile who, in the same century, forbade migrant sheep to enter the grain-fields, vineyards and meadows, thus robbing them of manure which could have increased the soil's fertility. (Many of the Castilian peasants, however, knew better than their royal masters, and made private arrangements for the sheep to pasture on the stubble of arable fields and in the vineyards after the vintage.) Further south in the Low Countries it seems likely that the peasants may have played a major part in the improvement of agriculture: the growing of industrial crops, horticulture and cattle-rearing provide ideal outlets for peasant skills. 'It is quite probable', Slicher van Bath has said, 'that most of the intensive cultivation came to be practised on small and medium-sized farms, with less than ten acres of arable land.'[20] But it is far less certain that the peasants reaped a just reward. The town regents of the Netherlands, on the whole, were kinder taskmasters than kings and nobles. But by the beginning of the eighteenth century the country had acquired a justified reputation as one of the most highly taxed countries in western Europe, and much of this bore down most heavily on peasants who had to pay the high capital and running costs of water-control works.

Not only in the Netherlands, but elsewhere, too, agricultural improvements often seemed ultimately to work against the peasants' interests. The sharecropper who increased production found that 50 per cent or more of the profits would be taken from the ground or snatched from the tree. In Jutland, where many peasants had turned increasingly to cattle-rearing in the fifteenth century, the profitable export trade in store cattle to Germany and the Netherlands was made a monopoly of the nobility. The introduction of the more productive three-course crop rotation into eastern Europe may have contributed in some small way to the enserfment of the peasantry by making it more possible to export grain. Even when the peasant did make money, he often did not have complete freedom to spend it as he chose. Sumptuary laws were passed in most west European countries, controlling the clothes that peasants were allowed to wear. In Flanders a law of 1545 forbade peasants to wear any velvet, coloured satin or damask, or gold and silver cloth; in Switzerland children were forbidden to wear satin, silk or plush; in Germany the lower orders had been obliged from 1486 to wear their cloaks over their head so that they could be distinguished from those who had the privilege of wearing them round their shoulders.[21] In Denmark ordinances were passed in the seventeenth and eighteenth centuries forbidding peasant wives and daughters to make clothes of costly materials or to wear ornaments of precious metal, while their husbands, it seems from inventories, were restricted to wearing black and red clothes – the outmoded colours of higher orders during the Renaissance.[22] To contemporary members of high society these regulations appeared to be well justified on both social and economic grounds, but in reality it might have been more generally profitable if some attempt had been made to respond to the challenge of increased demand. But that was impossible in what were still rigidly structured societies: the peasants could not be encouraged to want higher things than their lowly station merited.

The sumptuary laws are extremely interesting as they show that some peasants at least had a surplus of wealth to spend on finery; but the volume of the demand is unknown. What was the standard of living of the seventeenth-century peasant? Was it rising or falling? What did peasants eat? Were many of them starving? There are still only fragmentary answers to these questions. Artists and travellers provide some clues, though their judgments are only subjective.

27, 28, 29 The benefits of agricultural improvements did not necessarily reach the peasants: heavy taxes, monopolies and labour services meant continued poverty in many regions. *Below*, cave dwellings (France); *opposite above*, a primitive wooden shack (Holland); *opposite below*, the family of an Italian peasant.

There is more evidence to show that the standard of living varied greatly from household to household, from region to region, and from one period of history to another. Obviously, when so great a proportion of the European population was engaged in subsistence farming it is difficult, if not impossible, to come to any general conclusions. There were great variations from one farm to another. Even in some of the more advanced agricultural countries, there were farms where the seed-yield ratio still had not risen above the miserable medieval level of $1:4$, while a few farmers, like Rienck Hemmema of Hitzum, Friesland, were already obtaining an average ratio of $1:13\cdot6$ in the sixteenth century.[23] It does seem likely, however, that there were fewer general national advances in prosperity like those to which we have become accustomed, but far more local rises and falls, good years and bad, dependent largely on the vagaries of the weather. Even on Hemmema's farm the seed-yield ratio ranged from $1:7$ to $1:17$. The general productivity of agriculture was still so low that no country could totally guarantee a basic level of subsistence for the whole of its population every year out of its own resources. In the Netherlands, the emphasis on producing industrial crops, meat and dairy produce for the towns meant that between 13 and 14 per cent of the total amount of grain consumed annually in the seventeenth century had to be imported. Even some of the more prosperous merchants in the Netherlands seem to have lived quite frugally compared with present-day standards in the United States, where the average food intake in terms of agricultural cost is about eleven times higher than subsistence level.[24] 'Nothing is more ordinary', wrote one English visitor towards the end of the sixteenth century, 'then for Citizens of good accompt and wealth to sit at their dores, (euen dwelling in the market place) holding in their hands, and eating a great lumpe of bread and butter with a lunchen of cheese.'[25]

Outside the livestock farming areas, the composition of bread, its availability and its price, remained the main indicator of a community's well-being. Most peasants depended very heavily on grain crops, which provided fodder for working horses, one of the ingredients in ale, and flour for their main subsistence food. It is not known what peasants thought of the bread produced in neighbouring villages or in distant countries, for they very rarely, if ever, had occasion to sample it, but there is some evidence in the journal kept by that remarkable seventeenth-century seaman, Edward Barlow, the son of a peasant and himself a former farm worker, that he at least was very conscious of distinctions. When his ship had to victual in Denmark, he wrote: 'We had some of their country bread, which was black as bean bread, and some of their beer, which was as strong of smell as a thing that had hanged in the chimney seven years.'[26] White bread made from wheat was still a luxury in many parts of Europe, although it was becoming more common in some parts of England. Darker bread, made from rye, a less risky crop, was the staple food in most of central Europe. But the poor everywhere, and that in the seventeenth century meant the vast majority of people, often had to be content with bread made from buckwheat, a plant which will grow on poor soil, or heavy stringy bread or cakes made from barley or oats – 'a poore estate, God wot',[27] as William Harrison observed in 1577. Buckwheat, oats and barley were often eaten in the form of gruels or porridge. In times of dearth or famine the peasants had to make do with whatever substitutes they could obtain – ground peas, beans, tares or acorns or, in the south of Europe, chestnut flour, and in the extreme north, the bark of trees.

Yes, bark bread! That was what peasants in Sweden, Norway and Finland turned to in times of need up to a century ago. It was made from the pine or the silver birch. The thin membrane beneath the rough outer bark was scraped off, hung up to dry, and then beaten with a special flail with iron-tagged teeth to soften it before it was ground into flour. Although it contains some nourishment and holds no dangers for health, it is 'somewhat sour to the tongue',[28] according to one contemporary historian who has sampled bark bread cooked according to an extant recipe. Whenever this source of food became exhausted in serious famines, poor peasants were forced to eat whatever they could find – nettles, leaves of trees and bushes, grain husks, straw, moss and grass. From many different parts of Europe, including Sweden, France and Ireland, there are well-authenticated reports of corpses being found during famines with grass stuffed in their mouths, and from Finland of children chewing off their own fingers.[29]

'Hunger as such does not kill', D. E. C. Eversley has written, '– rather, it weakens the body and makes it prey to disease.'[30] The exact connections between lack of food and epidemics are very complicated, but it is clear that much disease in the seventeenth century, particularly infections of the lung and bowels, was caused by undernourishment or eating bad or harmful foods. Scurvy, caused by a lack of Vitamin C, was not only the worst scourge of seamen, but also killed many people inland whose diet was deficient in vegetables. Ergotism or St Anthony's fire, caused by eating blighted rye, killed some poor peasants and left many more with withered, blackened legs or arms, or completely limbless. The last European epidemic of ergotism occurred in Russia in 1888.[31] Cold winters reduced the spread of some bacteria, but had the adverse effect of making members of peasant families more prone to transmit diseases to each other by huddling round the fire. In times of severe famine, mortality could be very high. It is estimated that the population of Denmark declined by more than one-fifth between 1650 and 1660. Sweden also experienced its worst famine for fifty years in 1650. Famines occurred in the Iberian peninsula, particularly in Old and New Castile and Estremadura, in 1629–31, 1647–52, and 1683–85. In 1680, the population of Sardinia was estimated to have been reduced by a quarter. There were serious dearths in England in 1661, 1693 and 1697. Famine also occurred in France in 1693, killing many millions. In October of the previous year, the *intendant* of Limousin had written: 'The frost has finished off the few chestnuts and the little buckwheat that remained. The vines look as if they had been swept by fire.'[32] It was the poor who suffered most. The parish registers of Saint-Godard in Rouen show that, in the same famine, the number of paid burials doubled, while the number of charity burials increased twice as much.[33] When famine was linked with war, as it so often was, neither victor nor vanquished benefited. The losing nation was ravaged by death, destruction and disease, while the diversion of national resources often brought the winning country to the verge of famine, persuading even such a monarch as Louis XIV to sue for peace. Mercenaries, owing less allegiance to their paymasters than to their own appetite for plunder, robbed whole villages of their food and horses. Land went out of cultivation; the oxen had to be reyoked; and starvation intervened, as it did in whole regions of Germany during the Thirty Years War, when there were serious famines in 1624–25 and in 1637–38. It is estimated that up to one-third of the population perished.[34]

How often did these disasters occur and what effect did they have on mortality? Were there many regions like Beauvaisis which appears to have had famines every ten years or so in the last quarter of the seventeenth century with 10 to 15 per cent of the villagers dying of starvation or some concomitant disease?[35] Our knowledge of local history and epidemiology is still not far enough advanced to enable any certain judgments to be made. But it appears likely that, in addi-

30 An additional burden on the countryside's resources: mercenaries plundering a village.

tion to these major disasters, there were often local shortages in many different parts of Europe, their effects exacerbated by the dependence on grain crops, by lack of transport and by the operation of market forces, which produced increased shipments of grain away from areas of dearth, creating anger among the starving. Somewhere in Europe, almost every spring during the seventeenth century, there must have been some community, and sometimes a larger region or a whole country, shuddering on the brink of famine, faced with the choice of sowing seed to ensure its future survival or using it to bring some relief to the old and the young succumbing to starvation and famine-induced disease. It is little wonder that the harvest should have been awaited with such anticipation every year. For, once the tilling, the sowing and the harrowing had been done, there was little more that any farmer or peasant could do but to pray and to trust that some beneficent providence would blunt the cruel cutting edge of frost, cover the land with the warm ripening rays of the sun and delay the deluge which could leave the grain lying black and sprouting in

31 *The Ex Voto*, by Alphonse Legros. Religion has always been an integral part of country life, and even today, in parts of Europe, shrines can be seen by the paths and in the fields.

the fields. That is partly why, until very recent times, the hand of God has always lain so heavily on the countryside and the harvest has been attended with such rites of propitiation and celebrations of awe. Many medieval kneading-troughs carried the sign of the cross, and the peasant's wife crossed herself before she made her bread.

What saved at least the south of Europe from disasters even greater than those it actually experienced was the introduction of plants from the New World – one of the few fortuitous benefits that Spain provided for the poor. The prickly pear, brought back by the Spanish from the West Indies, could flourish even in rock crevices, providing a new source of fruit; but it was corn, or maize, which was the great saviour of the south. It was introduced into Spain at the beginning of the sixteenth century and spread fairly rapidly into parts of France and Italy. Even though the quality of its protein is somewhat suspect, and its lack of Vitamin B_2 can cause pellagra if the deficiency is not made up from some other source, its yield was two or three times higher than that of wheat. Ground into *polenta*, it was widely used as an alternative to bread in the south, where it flourished in the warm climate. It was not until the present century that a variety of corn suitable for north-west Europe was developed: there, the potato, another discovery from the New World, was increasingly adopted, though with much greater reluctance, in the eighteenth century.

Why was progress in agriculture so slow and tentative? One of the main reasons was that peasants, burdened by taxes, debts and rents, were unable to make the investments which were so sorely needed, not only in agriculture, but also in water control, land reclamation, rural transport, the building of bridges to replace ferries and the construction of better roads. During the seventeenth century something was done. There was continuing progress in the Po valley;

32 A fresco by Tiepolo, from the Villa Valmarana in Vicenza, which slightly exaggerates the fecund prosperity of a peasant family.

new estates were created and land reclaimed by the Venetian aristocracy; the first major attempt to drain the Pontine marshes near Rome was begun in 1623, and the embankment of a part of the river Tiber completed in 1678. Between 1630 and 1635 a start was made on draining the southern part of the Fens in East Anglia; land round Berlin was reclaimed under Frederick William, Elector of Brandenburg; and in the 1630s and in 1660 new fen colonies were founded in the peat-bogs of north Germany. On most of these projects, and on others in France, Denmark, Sweden, Poland and Russia, Dutch hydraulic engineers were in charge – Gilles van den Houten, Nicolaas Cornelis de Wit, Nicolaas van de Pellen and Cornelius Jansz. Meyer in the Pontine marshes, and Cornelius Vermuyden in the Fens.

These improvements, sponsored by monarchs, nobles and capitalists, were the bright jewels in a tawdry crown. Taking Europe as a whole, investment was only minimal. Even in the most advanced areas, far too much of the surplus was drained away in conspicuous consumption: in the Po valley 'churches and palaces absorbed the greater part'.[36] Further south, many of the great landowners remained almost completely indifferent so long as they could obtain quick profits from their estates. Some of their estates were vast: by 1660 half of the Roman Campagna was owned by six landowners.[37] There were large estates, too, in Sicily, in Naples, in Andalusia, preserved intact by mortmain and entail (legalized in Spain in 1505), many of which 'have been handed down undiminished right up to the present time'.[38] Some of the land was let out unimproved to shepherds, while in Sicily during the seventeenth century there was a great increase in the number of short leases which encouraged tenants, where they could, to wrench a quick profit from the soil, leaving it even more unproductive than before. Centuries of mismanagement and neglect caused a serious problem of soil erosion on many southern hillsides. As a result, avalanches thundered down, destroying roads and villages and diverting rivers which then flooded other areas.

In many parts of Europe there was a further diminution in agricultural investment from the middle of the seventeenth century when the general fall in grain prices lowered profits. This slump did not occur everywhere, for one farmer's loss is usually to another's benefit. The fall in the price of bread made it possible for townsmen to spend more on meat and wine, so that livestock and wine-growing areas benefited. But behind these secular changes there was a much stronger obstacle to improvement. Landowners were reluctant to invest while peasants still had so many rights, not only in the arable but also in the commons, while the peasants were reluctant to accept improvement because they feared, correctly in many cases, that it would mean higher rents or dispossession. That was why they fought so desperately against enclosure, and why the fishermen and peasants in the Pontine marshes breached the dikes in 1707, flooding the area again. This vicious circle was of no less importance in delaying agricultural improvement than was the vicious circle of the fallow in the actual fields, on which the propagandists of the English agricultural revolution concentrated so much fury.

To the Right Honourable the Lords Spiritual and
Temporal in Parliament assembled.

The Humble Petition of David Wilkins, Clerk, Rector of the
Parish of Hadleigh in the County of Suffolk, and of the Freeholders
of the Mannor of Hadleigh, who have a Right of Commonage
in Aldham and Boyne Commons, whose Names are hereunto
subscribed.

Sheweth   That the Poor of the said Parish are very numerous, and become a
great Burthen & Charge to the rest of the Parishioners.

That in order to make the same more easie, and that the said Poor
may be better provided, for; Your Petitioners (with Consent of the Dean
and Chapter of Canterbury, who are Lords of the said Mannor) have
agreed, that the said two Commons should be inclosed, and the Profits
arising thereby, imployed towards the Relief and Maintenance of
their Poor. But such Agreement cannot effectually be put in Execution
without the Authority of Parliament.

Wherefore Your Petitioners humbly pray Your
Lordships, that Leave may be given to bring in
a Bill for the Purposes aforesaid.

And Your Petitioners shall ever pray

D. Wilkins. Rector.   Isaac Everett
Geo. Serll   John Hayward
Robt Martin
John Darby   Joseph Gymor
Tho Martin   Tho Thrower
Robt Deason   John Bondall
Robert wife
Edw Buckenham   Joseph Glanfield

James Deason
John Godfrow
Matthew May
Thos Moss
William Smith
Henry White
John Gifford

III THE ENGLISH ACHIEVEMENT

The agricultural revolution in England – if we may still use that somewhat inaccurate but convenient term – was not entirely original: it depended partly on foreign example, just as the later industrial revolution owed a very great debt to Scottish inventiveness. But it was apparently so successful in increasing production, it was promoted with such self-acclaim, and it gave English lords such great security, wealth and power, that it attracted widespread attention in other parts of Europe. Of what did this so-called agricultural revolution consist? Let us first sweep aside a few possible misconceptions. The immense amount of detailed research carried out in the last thirty years into the origins and the course of the agricultural revolution has created a new picture. It would no longer be possible to maintain that the revolution was brought about only, or even mainly, by Viscount Townshend (1674–1738), of turnip fame; by Jethro Tull (1674–1741), the inventor of a seed-drill; by Robert Bakewell (1725–95), the breeder of Leicester sheep and Longhorn cattle; and by Thomas Coke, first Earl of Leicester (1752–1842), whose annual agricultural displays and sheep-shearings on his estate at Holkham, Norfolk, attracted aristocratic visitors from many parts of Europe. The agricultural revolution did not occur uniformly throughout the whole of England; it did not start in the eighteenth century and finish in the early years of the nineteenth century; it was not based entirely on the famous four-course Norfolk rotation of wheat, turnips, barley and clover; and machinery played little part in it. Equally, the parliamentary enclosures, which are usually linked with it, did not suddenly create a class of landless labourers out of the former free peasantry of England, who were then sucked into the factories of the new industrial towns in northern England.

Enough has already been said to indicate that change in the countryside does not occur so abruptly and homogeneously. The English agricultural revolution was far more complex, gradual and disparate, with its origins stretching back well into the seventeenth century

33 A petition to the House of Lords for enclosure in the village of Hadleigh, Suffolk (1728).

and in some cases into the previous century. In the main, it consisted of improvements similar to those which have already been noticed in the advanced agricultural areas of Europe: convertible husbandry, the floating of water-meadows, the replacement of the fallow by fodder crops like turnips, and the sowing of legumes, such as sainfoin, lucerne and clover, for temporary leys. There was also, possibly, a much greater use of the ancient practice of marling – the addition of clay to thin soils to improve their capacity for retaining moisture and manure – and of liming and manuring. (Although the nature of the soil cannot be fundamentally altered, it can be improved immeasurably over the course of many centuries by these means, constituting what some modern economists call a hidden capital.)

There were also great improvements in livestock-breeding in Britain during the eighteenth century. At the beginning of the century Britain still lagged behind many of its continental neighbours. The Dutch had their high-milk-yielding cows and their hard-working Frisian horses (now all black), which were probably first bred on a large scale during the sixteenth century in the Netherlands and in northern Germany; the Italians had crossed their native, lean, slow-maturing forest pig with the ancient eastern pig to produce a fatter animal; and Sweden, Saxony, Austria and France all had established flocks of merino sheep before 1768. But by the end of the century Britain was already exporting improved livestock, for which it was to become further renowned during the following century.

34 The face of the land before parliamentary enclosures: open fields near Cambridge in 1690. East Anglia was to become the heartland of agricultural progress.

35 *The Lincolnshire Ox* by George Stubbs (1724–1806). The eighteenth century saw great improvements in British cattle-breeding.

For these improvements in livestock-breeding an undue share of the credit has been given to the self-publicist Robert Bakewell of Dishley, Leicestershire, who bred a new type of Leicester sheep which gave more mutton, and a new strain of early-fattening Longhorn cattle, by breeding in. Bakewell used cattle which had already been improved by Webster of Canley, near Coventry, and sheep which had been improved by Joseph Allom. There were many other contemporary Midlands breeders who achieved results just as good as, if not better than, those of Bakewell, who carried his breeding of fat Leicester sheep to such an excess that some of them finished up not on the table, but with the tallow-makers. Bakewell's profits, like those of many other eighteenth-century English improvers, came far more from letting out his rams and bulls, whose value was increased by his self-publicity: his hall was hung with pickled specimens of his prize cattle.

36 Jethro Tull's horse-drawn seed-drill, designed in 1701 as a more efficient way of sowing seed than by the old method of broadcasting.

The face of England was not transformed overnight by these innovations any more than it was by parliamentary enclosures. The much-vaunted turnip, for example, was only suitable for light, deep soils, and many of the innovations could not be applied at all to some of the stickiest, coldest Midland clays, which could not be improved until the advent of cheap tile drains and the mole plough in the middle of the nineteenth century provided a means of sub-surface drainage. Machinery, in fact, played a relatively small part in the agricultural revolution. Jethro Tull's horse-drawn seed-drill was scarcely used at all until the late eighteenth century, and seed continued to be broadcast by hand.★ The introduction of the light, all-iron plough by John Brand, James Small and Robert Ransome in the 1770s and 1780s was far more important, as it allowed one man and two horses to do more work than two men and a boy with a team of six oxen had done before. Even so, farming still remained at a primitive level in parts of Britain throughout the nineteenth century. In 1850 there were still some peasant farmers in Sussex who 'clung to their two crops and a fallow for fear that any improvement would bring increased rents',[1] and others who used a wooden plough and six oxen to pull it. In places the ox team survived into the present century – there was still one at work in 1939[2] – while at least one example of the infield-outfield system of cultivation still existed in Ireland in the 1930s.

What part did the English peasants play in these developments? Until fairly recently, it was generally believed that they played no part at all, but modern research[3] and some neglected contemporary

★ Tull's invention was not original as it had been anticipated by John Worlidge in the seventeenth century; seed-drills were not used to any extent in England until the nineteenth century, and many of them were based on the improved adaptation of the French *agronome* Henri Louis Duhamel du Monceau (1700–82) – an interesting example of the international diffusion of agricultural innovation.

evidence show that this is not entirely true. W. G. Hoskins has traced the use of temporary leys in the open fields of Wigston back into the sixteenth century,[4] though this was possibly exceptional. It was far more difficult for the open-field peasant to introduce these improvements than it was for the man who leased or owned an enclosed farm. The common grazing of the stubble in the open fields made it necessary to secure the agreement of all peasants to any change of course, a difficult task when each individual's basic livelihood was at stake. Furthermore, the greatly increased amount of work involved in growing fodder crops might well have been beyond the capacities of a peasant and his family, or might have meant diverting labour from some more profitable activity. The ideal, for the peasant, remained subsistence farming or specialized production for the market in horticulture, viticulture, or the growing of industrial crops. Peasants in the Low Countries could live on an acre and a half of flax, but with mixed farming or grain-growing a much larger area was needed to provide a reasonable living. As a small farmer, the peasant was not equipped for large commercial activities.

The main innovations seem to have been introduced first by yeomen, gentleman farmers and substantial tenants. Eric Kerridge has been particularly assiduous in tracing back the channels of the revolution to their separate sources. From inventories, he has resurrected long-forgotten gentleman farmers and yeomen like Richard Hill, Miles Sinklen and John Reade, who had firmly established turnip-growing in Suffolk by the 1660s,[5] before 'Turnip' Townshend was even born. It is not known to what extent these changes were brought about by native ingenuity or by foreign example; but the similarities of soil and topography in East Anglia and the Low Countries – lapped by the same sea which has linked the countries more than it has divided them – made it possible for these innovations to be planted straight into the native soil of England, if indeed they had been gathered from some foreign source. The influence of merchants in these developments is a much-neglected study, but some of them were active in advertising foreign advances. There was a lively commerce between England and the Netherlands, and this may well have played some part in making English farmers more conscious of developments in the Low Countries. News of agricultural advances was brought home by squires and gentry, particularly by those royalists who sought refuge in the Low Countries during the English Civil War, and possibly also by those who had helped the Dutch against the

Spanish during the Eighty Years War. The most notable of these seed-carriers of the agricultural revolution was Sir Richard Weston (1591–1652), who wrote a book describing the advanced state of agriculture in Flanders and Brabant where he had lived from 1644 to 1649. On his return to his estate at Sutton, Surrey, he introduced fodder crops and the floating of water-meadows.

The role of the great landowners in introducing innovations was less important. Few eighteenth-century contemporaries accorded them a particularly high place. 'It seldom happens, however, that a great proprietor is a great improver,' wrote Adam Smith,[6] and his view has been confirmed by modern research. There were a number of obvious exceptions, like the Bedfords who played an active part for three centuries or more, from the draining of the Fens, through the breeding of merino sheep, to the building of model cottages for farm workers in the nineteenth century. But, on the whole, the main role of the English aristocrats was far more one of active encouragement, their essential contribution being 'the provision of fixed capital and the creation of a favourable environment for the adoption of better farming'.[7]

Why did the English agricultural revolution happen when it did? The lack of reliable national agricultural statistics and of a large number of separate farm accounts makes it difficult to give a satisfactory answer to this question in economic terms. It seems that the agricultural changes were first introduced at a time of falling grain prices, but it is possible that the increased demand for meat and milk products from the towns may alone have provided sufficient stimulus for farmers who practised the new efficient system of mixed farming: the population of London increased from an estimated 500,000 in 1660 to about 650,000 in 1714. Or possibly increased yields helped to lower grain prices. The subject is still open to debate. To a certain extent the changes arose naturally from other developments in society. During the second half of the seventeenth century and the first half of the eighteenth century, there was considerable expansion of large estates in England, made possible by a wide range of factors including marriages to wealthy heiresses, profitable investments, an increase in the opportunity for long-term mortgages, Irish rent-rolls, profits from West Indian sugar plantations, and government offices and sinecures. Many counties – not only those which were agriculturally unproductive – eventually came to have one or two dominant land-lords, like the Earl of Pembroke in Wiltshire and the Earl of Derby in Lancashire. Many of these great landowners were not particularly interested in agriculture itself, but most of them had sense enough to see that their own interests would be served by having tenants of reasonably sized farms who felt secure enough to make improvements so that they could farm successfully for the market. It was a peculiarly English compromise. The farmers' rise in profits allowed the landowner to raise rents gradually over the years and even to remit part of them in bad years, while the tenant knew that if he continued to farm successfully he would retain the tenure of his land, even though he might hold it only on a short lease. As one landowner's son told the tenantry when awarding prizes to his model farmers in the middle of the nineteenth century: 'It is by this friendly co-operation between landlord and tenant that the successful prosecution of industry and improvement can best be attained for your benefit as well as to mine.'[8]

37 The carefully planned and landscaped estate of Hampton Court, in Leominster, Herefordshire, around 1700.

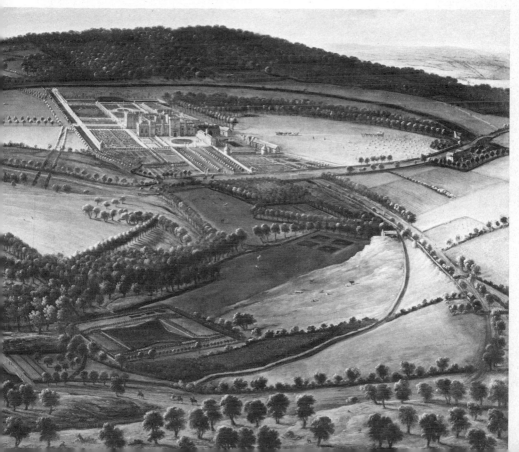

It was the perfect gentlemen's agreement (though who was the gentleman?) made at the expense of the peasant out of whose land these large estates had been largely created. The peasantry did not suddenly disappear from the stage of English history as a result of the Enclosure Acts in the second half of the eighteenth century, as was once believed; many of them had been gradually squeezed out of possession of their land from the beginning of the sixteenth century through fair and forced purchase, the engrossing of farms, the competition of commercial farming and the substitution of short leases for copyholds. Often, when some unscrupulous heir bent on boyish pleasures inherited his estates, many leaseholders soon became landless labourers, as is clear from the following verse of a ballad first printed towards the end of the sixteenth century:

> *Young landlords when to age they come,*
> *Their rents they will be racking;*
> *The tenant must give a golden sum,*
> *Or else is turned out packing;*
> *Great fines and double rent beside,*
> *Or else they'll not content be,*
> *It is to maintain their monstrous pride,*
> *While Mock-Beggar Hall stands empty.*[9]

38 *The Faggot Gatherers*, by Paul Sandby (1725–1809). It would be a mistake to think that the peasant vanished in England as a result of enclosure; the dream of self-sufficiency remained alive even into the present century.

The English Civil War brought forth a great crop of radical proposals for agrarian reform. There was much agitation for the conversion of copyhold tenures into freehold; Peter Chamberlen, a fashionable surgeon, proposed that a national bank should be established to lend money to the poor at a 5 per cent interest rate so that they might take over the forests and the commons: while the Diggers, led by Gerrard Winstanley, took direct action on All Fools' Day 1649, by starting to dig up the wasteland at St George's Hill, Surrey. There were also other, less celebrated, groups of Diggers at Wellingborough, Northants, and in parts of Kent, Essex and Gloucestershire. The Diggers have sometimes been dismissed as revolutionary idealists, but it is just possible that they may have been more practical than is believed. It was reported at the time that they had grown turnips – though whether that was for fodder or for the table is not known – and Winstanley himself, a failed merchant who became a herdsman, proclaimed that widespread poverty had been caused because the common land had lain unmanured for so many years. How was that to be changed, unless it was by the growing of the new fodder crops whose cultivation in another part of the country is definitely recorded only a few years later?

The Diggers' colony in Surrey collapsed after a year or so when its members were charged with disorderly and unlawful assembly. Previously, it had been attacked by a band of a hundred local farmers, which must almost certainly have included some small peasants, who were angered by this usurpation of their common rights. Local sufficiency rather than general equality was always the main hallmark of the peasant world. (In Wellingborough, however, the Diggers apparently received somewhat more sympathetic treatment from the local farmers, who gave them seeds to sow on their site.)

The Diggers' attempt to share out the wasteland, with or without improvement, among the poor, the landless and the younger sons, failed. Instead the Commonwealth came down firmly on the side of the encloser and the large landowner. Parliament, which in Tudor times had passed law after law against enclosure, threw out an Anti-Enclosure Bill proposed by Edward Whalley, one of the major-generals, in 1656. In the same year it confirmed the abolition of feudal dues for larger landowners, which had been ended previously by resolutions of both houses of the Long Parliament. After the Restoration, their abolition was finally reconfirmed by the Tenures Abolition Act of 1660, which allowed some minor dues to continue, such as frankalmoign, or the performance of spiritual services, and forfeiture of a traitor's lands to the Crown. Copyhold tenure, which was also feudal, was not abolished until 1925, although by then there were very few copyholders left to rejoice at its passing.

The domination of the landed classes in Parliament, and the diminution in the power of the monarch, allowed the former to use the legislature to speed up the process of agrarian change. Between 1730 and 1819 some 3,600 Enclosure Acts were passed, under which the arable strips in the open fields, the commons, the wastelands and the meadows of the village were shared out in enclosed farms and allotments among the occupants in proportion to their former holdings of land. These private Acts of Parliament were set in motion by a petition from local landowners, sometimes from just one or two of the wealthiest. The greatest number were passed in the 1760s and 1770s and during the Napoleonic Wars when there was a steep rise in the price of agricultural produce. It is not known with absolute certainty how much of the land in England and Wales was affected, but it is estimated that some six million acres, or about a quarter of the total cultivated area, was involved. (In Scotland two Acts of 1695 allowed run-rig strips to be consolidated into compact blocks, while another permitted the commons to be divided among its owners.)

Modern research has shown that the effects of the Enclosure Acts were varied, and different in many ways from what was once believed. They did not lead to a sudden exodus into the towns; more work was provided in most villages, temporarily at least, not less; the commissioners almost invariably shared out the land fairly; and in some villages the number of owner-occupiers may actually have increased.[10] The consolidation of scattered arable strips into compact fields had a number of important advantages for the larger farmer, as it allowed him to choose the crops he wanted to grow and meant that he had to waste less time in moving men and tools from one strip to another. The enclosure of fields and the partitioning of the commons made the selective breeding of livestock possible. Advantages, however, did not flow automatically from Enclosure Acts: in parts of the Chiltern Hills, for example, the three-course crop rotation continued to prevail,[11] as it doubtless did elsewhere, and some of the former commons remained enclosed but unimproved for many years. Furthermore, hedgerows may be rewarding to the naturalist and exciting for the huntsman (fox-hunting started to become a popular sport for the gentry about the middle of the eighteenth century), but

39 Surveyors at work on calculations for the enclosure at Henlow,
Bedfordshire (1798).

for the small farmer in particular they produce mixed benefits: it has
been calculated that the hedge round a five-acre rectangular field
occupies half an acre.[12]

It is possible to exaggerate the evils of these Acts. Relative over-
population and low wages may well have caused more suffering in
some areas, but, at the village level, where agrarian history must be
studied first, the changes that the Acts produced were different in
kind from any that had previously occurred in the long histories of
practically all these small communities. First, and most important,
enclosures compressed by law into a few short years alterations which
would otherwise have had to be made by force, chicanery or voluntary
agreement over many years, if not centuries, producing a drastic
contraction of the traditional village time-scale foreshadowing the
modern age. Secondly, they abolished most of the commons and the
wastelands which had been an essential element in the economy and
the way of life of small peasants for many generations. Thirdly, they
knocked the prop of custom away from those who could not prove
their legal rights to use the commons, and deprived them irrevocably
of any future claim. The enclosure award in Wigston Magna, made
on 17 November 1766, was, according to its historian W. G. Hoskins,
'one of the most momentous events in the long history of the village.
It transformed the physical landscape of the parish within a few years,
altered its farming beyond recognition, and changed the entire culture
and habits of the peasant community',[13] even though seven out of

ten families were already landless before the award was made. It would be false to generalize from this one example, as every village was a special case; but it seems clear that, in many small communities throughout the Midlands and the south of England in particular, the effects must have been no less drastic.

Consider for a moment what enclosure might have meant to the peasants in the village: the initial hints about the petition to Parliament, the rumours and uncertainties among them about the passage of the little-comprehended Bill, followed by the descent of outside commissioners, surveyors, clerks and solicitors upon the village world. After the award had been made there was frequently a storm of activity such as the village might never before have experienced. Squatters' huts on the commons were torn down for the last time; trees were felled to make fences, hedges planted, ditches dug; new roads were built and other roads and bridges were repaired; wealthier farmers had new houses built on their enclosed farms, and let off their former farmhouses in the village to two or three labouring families. Within a decade or so the physical appearance of many villages was totally transformed. Gone were the scattered strips in the huge open fields, and the vast stretches of unfenced common, and with them a way of life which stretched back for century after century. The social effects were neither uniform nor predictable. Some members of the lowest classes, like the squatters, may well have benefited by obtaining work which they had been unable to find before. Some may possibly have been able to exchange their rude hut of wattle and daub for two or three rooms in a former farmhouse. On the other hand, many of the established day labourers, living in a small cottage to which only customary common rights were attached, found themselves deprived of the latter and sometimes of the former, too. Some of the peasants who received a small allotment of land in compensation for their legally established common rights were persuaded to sell if they could not afford the heavy cost of fencing or if their holding was too minute or on such poor soil that it was unprofitable to cultivate it. Not all the peasants suffered. Some of the wealthier gained, by purchasing allotments which were added to their own farms, while even smaller peasants benefited if there was an opportunity to specialize. On the whole, the unknown number of smaller tenants and cottagers with only customary common rights seem to have suffered most. Their hopes of self-sufficiency were finally stretched to breaking-point on the lawful rack of increased efficiency and of higher profits.

40 George Stubbs, *The Reapers*. The dominant position of the English squire was greatly increased by enclosures.

The dream did not fade immediately. Doubtless it was still kept alive forlornly in the minds of many former peasants who had to take employment as day labourers, and it was sustained to a certain extent by the actions of some more benevolent lords, particularly in the north, who provided pastures where labourers might keep a cow. In the late eighteenth century the Earl of Egremont allowed each worker on his Yorkshire estate an allotment of three acres. 'When a labouring man can look up to a Resource of this kind,' wrote his steward in 1797, 'and has a warm cottage, and a Rood of land to grow Potatoes and other Vegetables, he is one of the happiest of men.'[14] True, but how common was this happy state? The dream of some self-sufficiency remained so strong – not unnaturally, as it had existed for so many centuries – that even towards the end of the nineteenth century it could still be one of the main rallying-cries for radical liberalism – Joseph Chamberlain's three acres with a cow.

The great lords, the squires and the landed gentry with large estates presided over a tamed countryside in the eighteenth century. There were few peasant protests during the passing of Enclosure Acts, which may be a tribute to the fairness with which the awards were made, but was also some indication of the extent to which the English peasantry, too, had been tamed by that time. The dominant position of the landed classes nationally, in Parliament, and locally, on the magistrates' bench, enabled them to transform the villages one by one. Each small community was isolated from its neighbours by its separate Act, a fact which doubtless sustained hopes of personal gain in many peasant minds until the often disappointing reality of their allotment shattered their deluded dreams. 'They give folks allotments instid o' ther rights', said one villager in Tysoe, Warwickshire, '– on a slope so steep, a two-legged animal can't stand, let alone dig!'[15]

The landed classes had a breadth of vision and a sense of business which distinguished them from many of the continental nobility. Among Spanish nobles it was a point of honour not to challenge their steward's accounts,[16] but English lords did not scorn to question and to check. Neither did they scorn all commercial and industrial enterprise: the fortunes of the Durhams, Northumberlands, Lonsdales, Derbys, Portlands and others were increased by profits from coal-mining. The third Duke of Bridgewater financed and helped to design the first truly man-made canal in England, from his coal-mines at Worsley to Manchester nearly ten miles away. Their interests in property development also helped to swell their fortunes. One writer

41 The gentry presiding over a transformed landscape: *Mr and Mrs Andrews*, by Gainsborough (*c.* 1748).

42 The Woburn sheep-shearing of 1804: not just a part of the farm work, but an opportunity to invite guests, exchange ideas on agriculture, and let out animals for high fees.

estimated at the end of the eighteenth century that a fifth of London had been built on ducal land in the previous two hundred years, much of it on leases under which the building reverted to the landowner. By 1866, out of 261 provincial towns, 69 were largely owned by great landlords and 34 by gentry.[17] The sale of land to railways also helped to increase their fortunes in the nineteenth century. By 1873, four-fifths of Britain was owned by seven thousand people, and there were sixteen men in England and Scotland with rents of over £100,000 a year from farmland.[18] On their estates, too, some of them showed no less enterprise. Their sheep-shearings and agricultural displays became internationally renowned. Coke of Holkham often had a hundred house guests and seven hundred to dinner. But these displays were not just idle ostentation. They helped to introduce new ideas to tenants and enabled the landowners to let their rams and bulls for high fees: the Duke of Bedford 'let above 70 South Down and new Leicester rams for above £1,000'[19] during his five-day sheep-shearing in June 1799. Agricultural societies also allowed them, and their tenants, to combine patriotism with profit by providing regular opportunities for displays of their prize animals and for the dissemination of ideas: the Dublin Society was formed in 1731, the Brecknockshire Agricultural Society in 1755, the Bath Society (later the Bath and West) in 1777, the Highland Society of Scotland in 1784, and the Royal Agricultural Society in 1838. Most of the English societies were dominated by the local landowners; there was very little co-operation between them, as there was in Prussia and Denmark where the main society in each province controlled a network of local societies.[20]

The landed classes, however, were not entirely men of good will. They had long revealed the unsmiling side of their faces to Ireland, where some three-quarters of the land was owned by Englishmen or West Britons – Anglo-Irish Protestant families. By the middle of the eighteenth century, £750,000 was being extracted annually in rents to line the pockets of absentee landlords in England,[21] while the interests of the Irish peasantry were increasingly sacrificed to profitable exports of wool, grain and beef, leaving the peasants to exist in squalid misery in filthy shacks on their small potato patches.

At home, too, they could be equally unscrupulous in defending their basic interests. Enclosures brought in new opportunities for thrills and spills in the excitement of the chase, and for the protection of specially reared game, to be shot with muzzle-loading guns. Many land-owners persuaded or forced tenants to plant broad hedgerows to provide jumps for horses and cover for the game, which they were legally forbidden to take even on their own land unless they were £100 freeholders, £150 leaseholders, or sons of squires. Foxes started to replace hares as the main quarry after faster hounds were bred by eighteenth-century hunts. Special game-rearing farms and hatcheries were established from the 1760s, the first probably being M. Dwight Pheasantries in Hertfordshire. The replacement of open common by enclosed farms and estates allowed the spring gun and the mantrap to be set – some toothless, others with two-inch iron teeth to pierce the poacher's flesh, and, most feared of all, the so-called 'bruisers', which did not penetrate the flesh but crushed the bone, leaving the victim a marked and easily distinguishable cripple for life. Game laws were passed which punished poaching with increasing ferocity. An Act of 1770 made poaching by night punishable by three to six months'

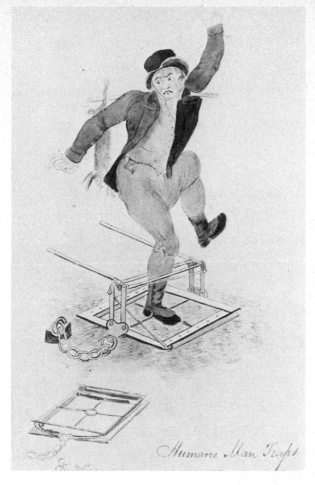

43 Other mantraps, less 'humane', might leave the victim a cripple for life.

Humane Man Traps

imprisonment; in 1803 a new law permitted poachers who offered armed resistance to capture to be sentenced to death; and from 1816 night poachers, even though unarmed, could be transported for seven years. With their armed gamekeepers and their trip guns, their high fences and their ha-has, some estates came to resemble military encampments, whose purpose was to protect the rights of lords and gentry to indulge in mass slaughter of specially reared birds. 'Whereas game had hitherto kept something of the wildness, and vagrancy, and careless freedom of Nature,' wrote the Hammonds, 'the woods were now packed with tame and docile birds, whose gay feathers sparkled among the trees, before the eyes of the half-starved labourers breaking stones on the road for half a crown a week.'[22]

What was the balance of national advantage in these agrarian developments? It is estimated that agricultural production in England and Wales increased by up to a half during the eighteenth century,[23] although the statistical evidence is too localized and fragmentary to speak with any certainty. In the first half of the century Britain became a net exporter of grain. Falling prices of grain at home led direct to Hogarth's *Gin Lane*, establishing a taste for dry London gin and slightly sweetened 'Old Tom' which was to persist into the sterner evangelical age at the end of the century, when specially bespoken hand-made drinking-mugs were defiantly inscribed:

> *William and Anne*
> *Think it no Sin,*
> *To drink a Glas*
> *Of British Gin.*
>
> 1791

The more balanced production of livestock throughout the year, made possible by the use of fodder crops and legumes, reduced the dependence on salted meat and salted butter, which possibly meant that less barley had to be used for brewing small beer – a weak drink with a low alcoholic content – which had once been consumed in prodigious quantities to slake the salt-induced thirsts of those who could afford to eat butter and meat. The lower prices of wheat gave the British an increasing taste for white bread which persisted after the sharp rise of grain prices in the third quarter of the century. Wheaten bread and fresh meat became the symbols of the somewhat legendary superiority of the English over continental nations, even though in the first half of the nineteenth century the masses rarely ate the roast beef of old England except at charitable dinners for the poor, and white bread seems to have been popular because it was the one food they could afford which could be eaten by itself with any pleasure. Famine and starvation were banished from England, except perhaps locally in a few exceptional years, though how far this was due to improved transport is not known. The larger agricultural production made it possible to feed a bigger population, which lived increasingly in towns, although it was not until 1851 that the urban population exceeded that of the countryside for the first time.

After the initial spurt of increased activity in the countryside during the enclosure movement, greater efficiency and harder work by those who remained on the farms gradually released more men for work

44 A bread riot of 1830: although larger agricultural production made it possible to feed a growing population, labourers' wages remained low.

in factories in the towns. Industry was stimulated by agricultural developments in numerous ways.[24] It is estimated that the increasing use of iron for ploughs and horseshoes accounted for 30 to 50 per cent of the total demand in England around the middle of the eighteenth century.[25] From the second half of the century, increasing prosperity among commercial farmers allowed them to spend more money on industrial goods: there were only one clock, six watches and one tea-kettle in one Scottish parish in 1760, but thirty clocks, a hundred watches and more than sixty kettles thirty years later. The agricultural revolution and the enclosures formed only one step – though perhaps a lengthy stride – on the centuries-long journey towards the kind of rural society which flourished in all the glories of Victorian high farming in the middle of the nineteenth century: a society with rich and dominant lords, prosperous large tenant and gentleman farmers, a relatively small surviving class of often poor peasant farmers, and a large class of exploited and crushed farm labourers whose smouldering

83

fury at their low wages had flamed into the rick-burning Labourers' Revolt of 1830 in southern England, East Anglia and parts of the Midlands. The revolt brought forth savage vengeance from judges in defence of property: 19 boys and men were executed, 481 transported to Australia and Tasmania, and another 644 imprisoned.[26] In the face of an increasing challenge from the revolutionary ideas of the town artisans and the desires of the new industrial magnates for cheaper food and power-sharing, the landed classes had by then turned the Irish side of their faces towards England. But the achievement on the land should not be minimized. As a result of these changes, English agriculture by 1870 was able to feed five or six times as many people as it did in 1700, mainly from much lower-priced home-produced food, with only about 20 per cent of the total male working population on the land.

There was, however, a debit side to these developments in the countryside. The ability to sustain a growing population, which started to increase considerably from the middle of the eighteenth century, was made possible to a considerable extent by gradually forcing the mass of people on to a new and initially unpalatable diet. The potato, native to Peru and other South American countries, was to play as vital a part in agriculture in the north and east of Europe as that other discovery from the New World, corn or maize, was to play in the south. Although the potato was already known in England in the sixteenth century, it was only necessity which forced people to adopt it as a food, first perhaps in Ireland, although that may have occurred later than was once believed,[27] and increasingly in England from the middle of the eighteenth century. Its misshapen tubers were not popular, as they were associated in the common mind with disease of various kinds; the resemblance of the flower to the nightshade made many people think that it was poisonous; and there was as much ignorance about cooking it as there was about the use of that oriental import, tea, which also reached the countryside about the middle of the eighteenth century and was sometimes mistakenly boiled by rural housewives as a herb with bacon. Like maize, the potato can feed about three times as many people as can wheat from the same acreage of land. Despite their initial reluctance, poorer people in England gradually came to accept the potato as part of their staple diet, particularly after grain prices started to rise. The dependence became even stronger in Ireland, where peasants consumed between eight and twelve pounds a day, supplemented by oatmeal and milk, to give a dull but nutritionally almost perfect diet.[28] Monoculture claimed its victims, as it always must, in the potato famine of the 1840s, when an estimated one million Irish men and women died of starvation or disease.

Farm labourers and their wives and children also often had to pay a high price for progress, with many of them working longer hours, on more days in the year, than they had done before. In some of the eastern counties of England, women and small children were organized into agricultural gangs which were let out to the highest bidder to perform the most onerous farm tasks – weeding, picking fruit, or clearing fields of stones. It was not until the Agricultural Gangs Act of 1867 that children under eight were prohibited from being employed in these gangs, though the law continued to be evaded for a number of years. Although a number of peasants and small farmers continued to exist or even to flourish, particularly in the livestock and horticultural regions, the basis of the old way of life had been destroyed in many areas of England by the beginning of the nineteenth century. By 1820, it is estimated, only two counties in England had more than 5 per cent of their total area in open fields.

45 *Seed-Time* (1854–56), by John Frederick Herring: the glories of Victorian high farming – though seed is still being broadcast by hand.

IV REPERCUSSIONS IN EUROPE

During the second half of the eighteenth century, agriculture became a more fashionable matter of concern than it had ever been before. It attracted the practical attention of such monarchs as Frederick the Great and George III, and the reforming zeal of enlightened despots such as Joseph II. Dozens of agricultural societies were formed even in some of the most backward and unenlightened areas of Europe. Thousands of experiments, many of them totally impractical, were conducted by enthusiastic amateurs among the aristocracy, and there was a plethora of publication, from simple manuals of instruction to learned tomes. That indefatigable publicist and horseman, Arthur Young, cantered through the length and breadth of France and Italy like some latter-day John the Baptist, preparing the unconverted for the coming of a new age by recommending improvements and the planting of turnips, sometimes in the most unlikely places. Italian poets celebrated the growing of rice and hemp in verse; the Marquis de Saint-Lambert addressed poetic eulogies to 'Turnip' Townshend in *Les Saisons*, published in 1769; in England itself, pastoralism was revived by Alexander Pope and Ambrose Philips. (The reality of English rural life was depicted by George Crabbe in *The Village*, published in 1783.) Painters like François Boucher and his pupil Jean Fragonard portrayed the Arcadian delights of a mythical bucolic life. The enlightened smiled upon the peasant and the serf and even in the doomed salons of Versailles, around the middle of the eighteenth century, the wives and courtesans forsook their elaborate costumes for simple peasant clothes on some days every week, while court masques depicted a fantasy world of milkmaids and shepherdesses.

◀ 46 French engravings depicting (*above*) summer and (*below*) autumn. The late eighteenth century saw a growing interest in agriculture among European revolutionaries, philosophers and aristocrats, but some of this concern was idealized; ladies of the court dressing up as milkmaids had no idea of the realities of country life.

There was a grim and burgeoning reality behind these ostentatious displays of high and cultured society. In the eighteenth century, and particularly from 1750, the population started to increase, for reasons which still remain partly obscure, not only in England but also in many other parts of Europe, at a rate which 'was very swift by the general standards of pre-industrial societies, and was often at its swiftest in areas most remote from rapid economic change'.[1] It is estimated that the percentage rate of growth per year in England and Wales between 1751 and 1801 was 0·80, while in East Prussia during the whole century it was 0·84 and in Hungary, between 1754 and 1789, 3·01.[2] The increased demand brought about a fairly general rise in grain prices from the middle of the century. As a result there was a new flurry of activity on the land: many countries tried to increase the arable area by enclosures, reclamation, conversion of pasture and the cultivation of marginal land, and attempts were made to introduce the new improved methods of farming and to popularize the potato.

England was the exemplar. Just as some members of the English gentry had squelched their way through the sheep-folds and the sodden polders of the Low Countries in the previous centuries, so now did some of the continental nobility turn envious eyes of admira-

tion towards England – and no more so than in England's nearest and greatest rival, France. From the middle of the eighteenth century many of the French nobility, influenced by the fashionable Anglomania, visited England to examine with their own, not entirely uncritical, eyes the splendid transformation which had been wrought in the countryside by English lords and large farmers. They included the Abbé le Blanc, Roland de la Platière, Dumont de Courset, and two members of the La Rochefoucauld family, the Duc de Liancourt and his son François de La Rochefoucauld. In 1784 the latter toured England, making the obligatory visits to Arthur Young, Robert Bakewell and the Townshend estates at Raynham. He was somewhat disconcerted to discover that enclosures and the agricultural revolution had not been so total as he had believed, being 'surprised, in a country so well cultivated, so enlightened, and so generally well conducted, to find so much common land and to find it even at the gates of the capital'.[3] But when he visited East Anglia – the heartland of the revolution – he was filled with almost unqualified admiration for the splendid agriculture, the prosperous and intelligent farmers of Suffolk, and the huge country houses, masterpieces of good taste, where the owner lived for eight months of the year,

48 *Above* Arthur Young (1741–1820), the great publicist of the English agricultural revolution.

47 *Left* Thomas Coke, first Earl of Leicester, inspecting his much-admired flock of Southdown sheep.

89

spending two months in London for the season and a similar length of time visiting a spa or staying with friends elsewhere. He came to the conclusion that 'farming is regarded as an honourable estate' because 'the highest in the land engage in it, and although they may do so as a pastime, they endeavour to make any profit they can'.[4]

Profit through agricultural improvement seemed to be the golden key which could unlock the door to an English world of prosperity. At home the La Rochefoucaulds, and many others like the Duke-King Stanislas and the Duc de Béthune-Charost,[5] introduced improvements on their estates. Marie-Antoinette started an English-style farm. The first agricultural society along English lines was founded at Rennes in 1757 and was followed by many others. Agricultural espionage and smuggling flourished: the French government broke the ban on exports of English sheep by paying for three Lincolnshire rams and six ewes to be smuggled into France by sea in 1763.[6] In 1785 the *intendant* of Paris distributed English turnip seed to members of the Royal Agricultural Society of Paris. With royal support, Antoine Parmentier (1737–1813) launched his campaign to encourage the eating of potatoes, but with only partial success, as many peasants still considered them to be suitable only for pigs. (Parmentier, however, secured a small niche of fame in the kitchen as the originator of the soup that bears his name.) After a royal proclamation of 1761 had offered inducements to land clearance, some attempts were made by individuals and by specially formed companies to bring waste land into cultivation. The most ambitious scheme was in Les Landes, a huge area of sandy dunes and streams, where shepherds on stilts watched their sheep in the malarial marshes. The work of draining and reafforesting this area was accelerated under Napoleon and finished in the nineteenth century.

The English achievement also acted as an irritant to French intellectuals, stimulating the growth of the highly elaborate and rigidly structured economic system of physiocracy. In 1756 the founder of the sect, François Quesnay (1694–1774), court physician to Madame de Pompadour, published in the *Encyclopédie* an article entitled 'Farmers', in which he pleaded for large-scale commercial farming of the English kind to be introduced into France. Two or three years later he published three versions of his *Tableau Economique*, a theoretical model of the economy with associated explanations and maxims, which sought to show how the economic sickness of society might be cured by a greater concentration on commercial agriculture, a

49 Shepherds
on stilts in
Les Landes in
south-western
France.

single tax on land rent and a general policy of *laissez-faire*. Quesnay boldly begins his explanation to the third edition of the *Tableau*:

Productive expenditure is employed in agriculture, grass-lands, pastures, forests, mines, fishing, etc., in order to perpetuate wealth in the form of corn, drink, wood, live-stock, raw materials for manufactured goods, etc. *Sterile expenditure* is on manufactured commodities, house-room, clothing, interest on money, servants, commercial costs, foreign produce etc.[7]

Physiocracy had a short-lived vogue in France. It had started to wane even before the death of Quesnay in 1774. Two years later one of its associates, Turgot, who as comptroller-general had brought in tax changes, was dismissed and his reforms repealed. 'Polite society talked physiocracy for a time,' says Joseph A. Schumpeter, 'but very few people outside took much notice of it except by way of sneering at it.'[8] The physiocrats had a bigger influence in stimulating agrarian reform abroad than they did at home.

The French were not the only Europeans who looked towards England as a model. With the personal encouragement of Frederick the Great (1712–86) – 'of all the arts farming is the greatest; without it there would be no businessmen, no poets and no philosophers'[9] – there was some agricultural progress in Prussia, particularly on large farms leased from nobles by commercial farmers round Berlin and on peasant farms producing for the market. Frederick sent agents into England to study their methods. Legumes and fodder crops were grown, there was more manuring and marling, and the English plough was introduced. Potatoes became a more common field crop, particularly after a dearth of grain in 1770; mangel-wurzels were grown for fodder and later imported into France and England; but it was experiments with sugar-beet which were ultimately to have the biggest consequences for European agriculture, by helping to release much of continental Europe from dependence on imported sugar-cane or from the use of honey as a sweetener. In 1747 a Berlin chemist, Andreas Marggraf (1709–82), succeeded in extracting sugar from beet. Unsuccessful experiments to produce sugar on a commercial scale were made in Silesia later in the century, and early in the following century Napoleon, in an attempt to beat the British blockade, decreed that some sugar-beet should be planted throughout the Empire. Although these experiments were little more successful, the French continued to cultivate sugar-beet after Napoleon's fall, and by 1836 were obtaining one-third of their sugar from this source. Sugar-beet spread into other mainland countries, including Prussia where it had originated, and by the middle of the nineteenth century European output equalled about one-sixth of the global production of cane sugar.

Frederick the Great also sought the aid of some earlier agricultural innovators in his efforts to increase the area of arable land. The services of Dutch hydraulic engineers were still greatly in demand throughout the whole of Europe: Frederick employed one of them, van Haarlem, to drain over four thousand acres of marshland in Brandenburg between 1773 and 1776, and took a great personal interest in the work. In all, Frederick is reputed to have reclaimed over 250,000 acres of

50 Adolf von Menzel, *Die Bittschrift*: the presentation of a petition to Frederick the Great. A nineteenth-century historical painting.

land and to have settled 300,000 colonists from other parts of Germany and from neighbouring countries. In 1770 he formed a Land Mortgage Credit Association in Silesia, subsidized by the central government, to lend money to landowners at low rates of interest. There were also some improvements in other parts of Germany. The Elector of Saxony imported and bred merino sheep. Agricultural societies were founded in many places during the second half of the century, two of the most important being the Thuringian Society, formed in 1762, and the Celle Society which was started two years later. Clover and lucerne were grown in parts of the Rhineland and sainfoin in Thuringia. But on the whole, apart perhaps from the regions round Berlin, the Mosel district, the Palatinate, and the Julich region, agriculture remained backward in many parts of Germany during the eighteenth century.

During the second half of the eighteenth century there was a re-awakening of agricultural interest in many other European countries, accompanied possibly in some of the 'less developed areas by a drift back to the land from the less prosperous towns.[10] The increased demands for food and raw materials to feed and to clothe a rapidly increasing population, the English example, the physiocratic message, and the Enlightenment, stimulated isolated individuals, societies and governments to seek a solution to the age-old cyclic problem of recurrent famine. The Trondheim Scientific Society, which also concerned itself with agriculture, was founded in Norway in 1760. In Switzerland, agricultural societies were founded in Berne, Basle and Zürich, while Hans Kaspar Hirzel's best-seller, the *Economy of a Philosophical Peasant*, published in 1761, revived interest in the peasant world. Rural problems were investigated by an Academy of Science founded in Portugal in 1779, as they were also by the Economic Societies of Spain. In Italy the famous Accademia dei Georgofili was founded in Florence in 1753. Further south in Naples, Antonio Genovesi (1712–69), professor of political economy from 1754 to his death, 'acted as the pivot of the reform movement,' says Venturi, the historian of the Enlightenment in Italy, 'and it is to his group that we must trace those who attempted to create agrarian societies, to improve specific cultures (oil, silk, grain, etc.), to establish a lively contact with the Georgofili Academy in Florence and the Venetian Societies, to create and to criticise the government's economic policy'.[11]

The rays of the Enlightenment stretched out to stroke, however briefly and gently, some of the most backward areas of western Europe. In Calabria from 1770 Domenico Grimaldi, 'taking as a model Swiss stock-raising and northern Italian irrigation',[12] experimented with fodder crops and new methods of producing silk and oil. In eastern Europe the Enlightenment shone less brightly. In Russia, a few progressive landowners started to experiment with forage crops towards the end of the eighteenth century, and the government tried to encourage the cultivation of potatoes from 1765, though little progress was made until the middle of the nineteenth century, following the famine years of 1839 and 1840.[13] In 1756 a Free Economic Society was founded in St Petersburg, which concerned itself with agricultural problems.

European landowners in the eighteenth century were also stimulated to enclose commons and wastelands and to consolidate scattered holdings into compact farms. As in England, there were already many enclosed farms and commons in different parts of Europe, some of which were of considerable age. In Normandy the enclosure of arable land had been proceeding since the sixteenth century, and elsewhere in France, as we have seen, some commons had already been divided up. But from the middle of the eighteenth century, with the English example in mind, the state tried to encourage enclosures by a series of edicts. In 1761 a royal edict exempted improved land from taxation for a decade. Between 1767 and 1771 other edicts allowed commons to be enclosed in many provinces of France, with the owner of seignorial rights taking one-third as his share. Commercial companies and some large landowners farming for the market, whose estates were already large and unified with woodlands to provide the necessary fencing, took advantage of these opportunities to enclose, but many nobles were too poor to afford the capital investment; others, as in the neighbourhood of Lyons, placed a higher value on their hunting rights; and many lords in the central provinces and Dauphiné preferred to retain their rents from peasants for the use of common pastures.[14] In parts of Germany, too, state regulations governing the enclosure of commons started to be issued from 1750, but enclosure and consolidation proceeded very slowly and patchily; there were exceptions in some states dominated by the nobility, like Mecklenburg, where peasant evictions (*Bauernlegen*) were so extensive that by the end of the century an estimated two-thirds of the province was in large estates.

Neither the English agricultural revolution nor the enclosure movement could be transplanted direct into foreign soil. The former withered in the cold blast of indifference among so many large landowners and the heated suspicions of peasants; the latter was obstructed by noble aversion to investment, the authorities' fears of disturbances and peasant stubbornness. Changes had not been forcibly imposed upon England, but had arisen naturally from the development of society during the previous centuries, or had been gathered abroad, planted and nourished carefully until they flourished in the native soil. Foreign reformers who broadcast the seeds of improvement on European soil found that many of them fell on stony ground. Agricultural change could not be imposed on backward societies with their serfs, their feudal dues, and their restrictions of individual freedoms. Even such a basically conservative philosopher as Christian Garve (1742–89) realized that serfdom, which still existed in so many parts of Germany, had become an obstacle to progress. His arguments, and the counter-arguments of the German nobility, have a contemporary ring: he claimed that the peasants' backwardness, laziness and ignorance were a result of the social structure, while the nobility asserted that it was their inherent incapabilities which made it necessary to retain the allegedly patriarchal system.[15] The body of society had to be prepared for the transplant if it was not to be rejected. The structure had to be changed; the circulation of ideas, of labour, of capital had to be quickened. As the eighteenth century drew to its close, the need for change in society as a whole assumed an ever-increasing importance. The *ancien régime*, worm-eaten and rotten though it was, was kept together by centripetal force; perhaps it might be toppled by a push from above or from below. Philosophers and economists provided the rationale of change; enlightened monarchs and statesmen tried to introduce it, with varying degrees of success; but it was sometimes enemy generals who finally drove the lesson home.

The agrarian changes made towards the end of the eighteenth century and in the early years of the nineteenth century were to have a long-lasting influence on the development of national societies, and their effects have persisted in some cases to the present day. One of the most striking transformations occurred in Denmark, where the peasants had been far more oppressed than they were in the rest of Scandinavia or in many other countries of north-west Europe. From the middle of the fifteenth century onwards the nobility, particularly in the eastern islands of Lolland and Zealand, had started to impose, under German influence, a limited form of serfdom on their tenants by binding them to the soil. Although *vorneskab* was abolished by Frederick IV in 1702 for all peasants who had been born since his accession three years earlier, his limited reform had had little time to take effect before even more onerous obligations were imposed by the new king upon practically the whole of the Danish peasantry, with the exception of those in Bornholm, and in Schleswig-Holstein, which already had a large number of serfs. The small number of peasant freeholders who may have owned 4 to 5 per cent of the land were also exempt. In 1733, in the middle of the agricultural depression, Christian VI decreed that no peasant between the ages of fourteen and thirty-six (later extended from four to forty) was to leave the estate on which he had been born, and the nobility were given the right to select those peasants who would serve in the army for an

51 Changes in the agrarian structure of Denmark led to a nation of small freeholders, many of whom specialized in dairy farming.

eight-year term. The *stavnsbånd* greatly increased the power of the nobility, about a quarter of whom may have been of foreign origin, mainly German. Labour services were increased, sometimes to three or four days a week; corporal punishment was common; and the right to choose militiamen gave the nobility a lever with which they could bend the peasants to their will. In 1746 it was decreed that peasants who had served their time in the army had to return to their estates; there was to be no escape for the recalcitrant.

By the end of the century, however, the agrarian structure of Denmark had started to be totally transformed, so that the country, released after 1721 from its long series of exhausting wars with its rival Sweden, could take full advantage of the rising prices for farm products and of the profitable export opportunities to other war-torn European nations. Denmark was the only country in western Europe which made a direct transition from serfdom to state-supported freehold farming, establishing a pattern of progressive agriculture and peaceful change which has persisted to the present day. The changes were imposed from above, mainly by the group of enlightened, landowning statesmen and administrators who exercised real power during the reign of the feeble-minded Christian VII, who came to the throne in 1766 and was replaced in 1784 by his sixteen-year-old son, Frederick, who acted as regent until his father's death in 1808. Initially, the reformers experimented on their own and on the royal estates. Count Stolberg, steward of the estates owned by the widow of Christian VI, persuaded her to commute labour services for money rents.[16] In 1767, Count von Bernstorff (1735–97), one of the leading reformers, started to make enclosures on his own estate. In 1786, a Land Commission was set up under the chairmanship of Count Reventlow (1748–1827), who had studied agriculture at first hand in England. The landlord's right to inflict corporal punishment on peasants (though not on labourers) was abolished in the following year, and on 20 June 1788 *stavnsbånd* was ended, making the peasant 'a free citizen', as the Column of Liberty in Copenhagen proclaims. As a result labour services were gradually commuted for money rents. Earlier in 1781 an Enclosure Act had been passed to encourage the consolidation of strips of land in the open fields into compact farms. Peasants were encouraged to move out of the old nucleated villages into their own homes on enclosed farms by government loans at low rates of interest, so that by 1820 over half of Denmark's farmers had become freeholders.

It was a remarkable achievement which, within a century, had transformed the social structure of the nation and the face of the countryside by creating a new kind of relatively small farmer orientated to the market at home and overseas. But the changes had their reverse side. The ancient village community of peasants was gradually destroyed; cottagers suffered greatly, particularly in the slump following the Napoleonic Wars; and a new class of landless labourers was created. (It was not until the 1890s that the government started to create thousands of smallholdings out of large estates and by the conversion of remaining leaseholds.) These reforms were carried out by autocrats who believed in charity for the poor, but had little real sympathy with the landless, and even less with the peasants in the other part of the kingdom – Norway – who were demanding the abolition of the Danish corn monopoly, a reduction of some of the thirty-six taxes they were forced to pay, and a stricter control over officials' fines and fees. A revolt in south-eastern Norway in 1786–87, led by a peasant, Christian Lofthus, was soon crushed. After his capture, Lofthus was imprisoned – chained to a block – in the fortress of Akershus, his sentence of life imprisonment finally being confirmed twelve years later, two years after he had died.[17] By the end of the eighteenth century a very different kind of social structure had developed in the Norwegian countryside, with a much larger class of cottagers and landless labourers (possibly half of all workers on the land), and a smaller class of richer freeholders and larger tenants, concentrated particularly in the wooded areas, where incomes could be supplemented by forestry. The government tried to encourage enclosures and land clearances, but a full-scale programme of enclosures was not instituted until after the break with Denmark – in 1821, and again in 1857.

In France, despite the burning of some châteaux, the confiscation of Church and *émigré* property, and the decrees of the National Assembly, the Convention and the Jacobins, the ultimate changes in the agrarian structure were much less extreme than they were in Denmark. The events which followed the *Grande Peur* of 1789 occurred in a much larger and more variegated country, stretching from the North Sea to the Mediterranean, with great regional variations in land ownership, social structure and agricultural techniques. The nobility may still have constituted an estate, but they were by no means a uniform class. They ranged from the great nobles who were rich enough to while away the hours in Paris and Versailles to those round Auch, discovered by Arthur Young on his travels through France, who were so poor that they had to plough their own fields. The amount of the land owned by the nobility also varied greatly from one region to another, from an estimated one-quarter in Burgundy, Picardy, Artois and Béarn to not much more than one-tenth in Dauphiné, Quercy and Limousin.[18] Many of the nobility, like the bourgeoisie, were absentees, but there were also a number who lived mainly on their estates, some for reasons of economy and others, like the *agronomes*, in the hope of improving their estates and profiting thereby. (These included women, like the young Viscountess du Pont, sister of the Duchess of Liancourt, who, according to Arthur Young, probably grew more lucerne than any other person in Europe.[19]) There was an equal diversity, as we have seen, in the peasant* world, with its wealthy *fermiers*, *laboureurs*, *manouvriers* of varying degrees of relative affluence and poverty, and landless labourers, who may have constituted some three-quarters of

* French and English rural terms, though apparently similar, have very different meanings: peasant is not equivalent to *paysan*, labourer to *laboureur*, or farmer to *fermier*.

52 J.J. Boissieu, *Peasants Begging* (1780): by the eighteenth century, many French landowners were extracting invented 'feudal' dues from the peasants, which brought about an increase in poverty.

the rural population in the region of large farms in Flanders and Picardy – the great granaries of the north – though they often rented a little patch of land for their own subsistence. Some of the wealthiest peasants did not own their own farm but rented it, frequently leasing out other land they did own to poorer peasants. Peasant ownership varied greatly from region to region, but they may have owned in aggregate about one-third of the land, much of it in the poorer and the more remote areas. Sharecroppers were possibly the most numerous class. It is not surprising, in view of this great diversity, that there should have been something less than a community of interests among the peasants; but, as that great historian Georges Lefebvre pointed out long ago, the peasants might have been opposed in many interests, but they were united in their hatred of seignorial rights – particularly the *banalités* of the mill, the oven, and the olive- and the wine-press, which could have such disastrous consequences on the vintage, and the *droit de chasse*, which had made the hunting of game an exclusive privilege of the nobility by a royal decree of 1669.

53 A French print of 1789: the peasant carrying the clergy and the nobility
on his back.

Game laws were even more restrictive than in England. In some places, peasants were forbidden to weed or hoe, lest the young partridges should be disturbed; to mow hay before a certain date, which was so late that it ruined many crops; or to use night soil as manure in case the delicate flavour of the partridge was spoilt.[20] With the rise of prices from about 1730 and the increasing number of lawyers and businessmen buying themselves into land, there seems to have been a tendency for many seigneurs to try to extract even more money from the peasantry by reviving old dues and inventing new ones. Even though some of these dues may have been feudal in origin, by the eighteenth century they had become, in the words of A. Cobban, nothing but 'a commercial racket'.[21]

By 1789 new techniques had already been introduced on some French estates and farms. Change was much less extensive than in England, for a variety of reasons including the indifference of many large landowners, the cautiousness or conservatism of peasants, the restrictive effects of short leases and *métayage*, and the general in-applicability of the reforms in the large mountain, Mediterranean, vine-growing and tree-crop regions. There were both big farms and small, many of them already so minute that they could not provide a basic subsistence, but peasant ownership of land had long been accepted in principle by the law, though in practice it did not always survive the testing time of court action. On the whole it seems fair to say that all classes in France were far more firmly wedded to the idea of ownership of land in absolute terms than they were in England, and that when they thought of use it more often meant feudal dues or common grazing rights than agricultural improvement.

Agriculture – or its failure – was one of the immediate causes of the French Revolution. The disastrous grain harvest of 1788, followed by another poor harvest in the following year, sent the price of bread soaring by 100 per cent nationally on a week-to-week comparison and by 200 per cent in some places, and this at a time when workers spent about half of their income on bread; the drop in demand for industrial goods may have reduced production by half, leading to widespread unemployment.[22] The peasants, except for some of the largest, were also badly affected because they had no surplus grain to sell and often insufficient for their own needs. As always happens in times of dearth, there was a much greater movement of grain from region to region and out of the countryside into the towns. The

54 Building a road under the state corvée in eighteenth-century France.

peasants, many of them half-starved, saw the loaded grain carts disappear along the roads they had helped to build under the state corvée, just as Irish peasants were later to see vast quantities of grain shipped out of Irish ports to England in the great famine of the 1840s. There was a series of isolated and sporadic attacks on châteaux and nobles, which increased in ferocity in July and August 1789, after the fall of the Bastille, when much of the countryside was gripped by the *Grande Peur*. A rumour arose simultaneously in different areas that hired brigands in the pay of the nobility were being sent to restore law and order in the countryside. More châteaux, and their documents and papers, were burnt; nobles were attacked, and their wives and daughters raped. (Not all châteaux were burnt, and neither did all the nobility emigrate or lose their heads.)

It was mainly through fear of further peasant risings that the National Assembly somewhat reluctantly abolished feudalism in France on 4 August 1789. Personal serfdom, seignorial courts and tithes all disappeared, but the assembly, which included many property-owners, was unwilling to abolish seignorial dues and decreed that these should be redeemed by payments over a number of years. It was not until 1793, when peasant support was needed for the war against England, that the dues were abolished. In these respects the changes were revolutionary, but the alterations in land ownership seem to have been far less radical. Land owned by *émigrés* and by the Church, which held about 6 per cent of the total, was put up for auction. It is thought that the wealthier peasants, the bourgeoisie, and even some of the nobility, through the help of nominees, benefited; but the smaller peasants, the landless and the sharecroppers, gained much less. It has been estimated (though the conclusions are rather tenuous) that between 1789 and 1815 the number of small peasant owners may possibly have increased by a million or more through the purchase of land and other means, although the total amount the peasantry cultivated did not increase substantially.[23] The Constituent Assembly tried to help larger, commercial farmers by authorizing enclosures in all parts of the country, with certain safeguards to protect other peasants; and in 1792 and 1793 laws were passed allowing the commons to be divided up, which should have been of some benefit to the landless. It is not known how many enclosures and divisions of commons were carried out, but it seems likely that neither were extensive. The old way of life and peasant attitudes were deeply entrenched in France, so that common rights and *vaine pâture* – the right to graze cattle and sheep on the stubble and the fallow from the harvest to the following February – persisted in some parts of France well into the nineteenth century. The Revolution brought about no radical alterations either in agricultural techniques or in land ownership. It was a victory for the property-owner. France remained a country of large farms – some in the north are now over a thousand acres – and of small peasant holdings as it had been before, deeply conservative, and with a much greater respect for property than for agricultural improvement.

Agrarian reform in Prussia produced a very different kind of social structure which was to be fateful for the future course of German history. When Frederick the Great came to the throne in 1740 he abandoned the previous policy, which had lasted nearly a century, of trying to curb the powers of the nobility by restricting their political independence, expanding royal estates, allowing the middle classes to rent royal land and making the nobles in East Prussia pay their share of taxes. His isolated attempt in 1763 to abolish serfdom in Pomerania by decree was soon rescinded in face of noble opposition.[24] Although he continued his predecessors' policies of trying to halt peasant evictions and preventing harsh punishments of serfs, his policy was generally designed to aid the nobility, whom he needed to staff his armies and to help run the state machine. He encouraged agricultural improvement, subsidized mortgages, helped to consolidate noble estates in the east by an edict of 1751 which allowed owners to enclose their own land and a share of the commons, forbade, with a few exceptions, the sale of noble land to the middle classes, and restricted succession to a single son. In spite of this official patronage and of unofficial benefits, such as the army practice of giving soldiers lengthy leave to work as labourers on the estates of noble officers, many of the nobility remained poor, working their unimproved lands with forced labour (which usually meant three days for the peasant every week) and using the peasants' younger children as domestic servants, on the grounds that it helped to socialize them. It was said that the nobility exercised 750 separate rights of control and extortion, ranging from approval of a peasant's choice of wife to a tax on bees. 'The aristocracy of Prussia', wrote Baron vom Stein in 1808, 'is a burden to the nation, because the members of this caste are found in great numbers, are poor and full of claims, receiving emoluments, occupying official posts, and demanding privileges and precedence of every kind.'[25] As a result of foreclosures on mortgages, the middle classes had already started to take over some noble estates towards the end of the eighteenth century. By 1800, 9 per cent of proprietors of noble estates in the Electoral Mark were members of the middle classes.[26]

The defeat of the Prussian armies by the French at the Battle of Jena in 1806 drove home the need for a thorough reform of society at all levels. In 1807, as Prussia's leading minister, Baron vom Stein (1757–1831) introduced reforms which freed the nobility by allowing them to engage in trade and industry and to enter the professions, freed the middle classes by allowing them to buy land, and freed the peasants by abolishing serfdom on noble estates and allowing them to buy and sell land. These reforms were extended in 1811 by Prince von Hardenberg (1750–1822), whereafter peasants with hereditary tenures were allowed to become owners of their land by paying twenty-five years' rent or by giving up one-third of their holding to the landowner (or half, if they had only a life lease).

Unfortunately for Germany, these mild reforms did not have a fully liberalizing effect, particularly for many peasants. The nobility fought a long delaying action, so that the agrarian changes were not completed in some cases until the middle of the nineteenth century, when cottagers were also freed from the obligation to work on noble estates. On some of the more remote estates in the east, nobles managed to retain their judicial power to 1918. Although poor nobles continued to be a problem, many were able to increase the size of their estates greatly by these reforms, though the total extent of their gains is still disputed. It is generally estimated that through commutation of tenures, purchases, and enclosures of commons, the nobility's share of the land increased by some two and a half million acres. The extent of peasant gains and losses is even more contentious. Some of them may have increased the size of their holdings through the division of the commons, but it is generally agreed that many of them degenerated into landless labourers, particularly in the nineteenth century after the nobility started to increase still further the number of sheep farms, as had been done earlier in England and in Spain. The Junkers remained firmly established in their large houses with their cannons, souvenirs of war, at the iron gates, masters now not of serfs but of their respectful labourers, who were summoned to work each morning by the tolling of a bell on the large estates in the cheerless plains. The increasing tendency among the nobility to marry into the middle classes produced much more formidable combinations of toughness and shrewdness, in men such as Bismarck.

Agrarian changes in the rest of Germany varied very greatly from state to state, just as did the kinds of agriculture practised. Levels of achievement ranged from some of the most advanced commercial farming, in the neighbourhood of large towns, to some of the most unprofitable in remoter areas where the peasants had to supplement their income by making wooden clocks, dolls and musical instruments. But in all states serfdom had been abolished by 1848. In some principalities it had been abolished before the Prussian reforms, as in Baden in 1783 and Holstein in 1800; in the Rhineland and south-west Germany, where the number of serfs was small, it had been ended by Napoleon; while in Bavaria, where it had been more important, personal serfdom was ended in 1808 and labour services ten years later.

In the Habsburg dominions to the south-east the Enlightenment, which burned brightly enough in Vienna, faded to a weak, winking star when viewed from the furthest boundaries of some noble estates unparalleled in western Europe since medieval times for their vastness. In the eighteenth century, the latifundia of the greatest Hungarian nobles were usually from twenty thousand to fifty thousand acres. 'A single family', says C. A. Macartney, 'might possess many such units: thus the Eszterhazy family, the greatest of them all, owned at one time seven million Hungarian acres.'[27] The Schwarzenbergs in Austria and the Lobkowitzes in Bohemia were also landowners on a huge scale. In the eighteenth century, a few of these landed magnates attempted to replace medieval by modern means of cultivation on their estates, while in western Hungary some of the largest landowners started to import cattle from Switzerland in an effort to improve their own herds. There were even a few enlightened owners, like Count Sporck, who reduced the labour services of the serfs on his vast estates in north-east Bohemia, founded hospitals, and provided charity for the poor.[28] But they were exceptional and most of the nobility, large and small, looked on the forced labour of their serfs as part of the natural order. As one Hungarian noble wrote: 'God himself has differentiated between us, assigning to the peasant labour and need, and to the lord, abundance and a merry life.'[29]

In the 1770s Maria Theresa (1717–80) introduced reforms cautiously, province by province, regulating the dues and the number of days' labour (robot) that peasants had to provide for their lords. From 1775 dues and services on royal estates were commuted for money rents. Her son Joseph II (1741–90) imposed much more radical reforms, culminating in his decree of 10 February 1789, which abolished all labour services in return for a rent fixed in relation to the peasant's gross income. This measure aroused intense opposition among landowners, particularly among the powerful, conservative Hungarian nobility. It was a hopelessly impractical reform, as many peasants still lived at subsistence level, tilling their unimproved lands to reap nothing but a miserable medieval-level yield of grain. As William H. McNeill has said, 'even professional bureaucrats could not squeeze blood from a turnip nor money from peasants who had no cash income'.[30] The measure was repealed in Hungary just before Joseph's death and in the other provinces by his brother, Leopold II, who succeeded him.

55 Eighteenth-century view of a vast Polish estate; in the distance, seen through the trees, is the villa of Princess Isabella Lubomirska.

The enlightened effort to speed Austria along the path of agrarian progress by abolishing serfdom and diverting some of the peasant-created wealth into the exchequer of the centralized state, so that it would be strengthened to resist the threat from Prussia, had been blocked by the immovable power of the landed magnates whose estates in Hungary had been held inalienably since 1351. It was not until the nineteenth century, when the river steamboat and the railroad had produced new opportunities for exporting farm products, particularly wool and sugar-beet, that some of the larger nobility completely reversed their previous policy and tried to force the deeply conservative Austrian government to abolish inefficient labour services so that paid day labourers could be employed instead. Fearing peasant insurgency in 1848, the central government freed the serfs, but the social structure was scarcely changed and Hungary remained a country of huge latifundia, peasant smallholdings, and an increasing number of landless labourers.

In the endless plains, forests and steppes of eastern Europe, the twin beacons of English pragmatism and continental Enlightenment became almost totally obscured. In Poland before the partitions King Stanislaw August (1732–98), supported by a few enlightened nobles, tried to introduce some mild reforms – the gradual emancipation of the serfs, and the freeing of nobility to enter trade and of the bourgeoisie to own estates. But what chance did he have of success when his country was still dominated by feudal overlords like Prince Karol Radziwill, Lord-Lieutenant of Vilno, who had his own court and private army and estates which totalled half the size of Ireland?[31] Seeing how England arranged its affairs on a visit in 1754, the king wrote home pathetically: 'Would to God we do the same!'[32] But it was not to be. Poland was swallowed up by Prussia, Austria and Russia, which meant that the peasants remained enserfed for another century at least, being freed in the Austrian provinces in 1848 and in Russian Poland in 1864, when they were allotted on average four times as much land as the Russian peasant to strike a blow at the rebellious Polish nobility.

It was in Russia that serfdom reached its most spectacular extremes in the context of a barbaric society where malefactors were hanged by the ribs and serfs were banished to Siberia at a nod. In the early

56 In Russia, where serfdom was carried to brutal extremes and Peter the Great himself set a harsh example, rebels were hanged by a hook through the ribs.

years of the eighteenth century, under Peter the Great (1672–1725), the nobility was given new powers and responsibilities. Meanwhile the serfs were weighed down with new burdens of oppression, the poll-tax and compulsory military service, while many formerly free peasants in south and central Russia were enserfed. Peter the Great created a unique service state in which all people, both high and low, were expected to bend to his immense will and huge determination. Members of the nobility, carefully graded as a class by his Table of Ranks of 1722, were forced to serve him as army officers or as bureaucrats in return for possession of the land and the possession of their serfs. Peter himself set an example for the suitable treatment of serfs by giving thousands of serf families to nobles in return for special services; others he used to build roads, harbours, canals, and the new capital of St Petersburg (now Leningrad), founded in 1703, one of the most beautiful and best-planned cities in the world and one which, like some other very recent monuments to culture in other parts of eastern Europe, was constructed by forced labour. One Soviet historian has calculated that the labour services for the average peasant household in the eighteenth century may have amounted to between 125 and 187 days a year.[33]

Only a few significant features of the history of the peasants and serfs in eighteenth-century Russia can be highlighted here.[34] In spite of some industrialization, Russia remained a predominantly rural nation; as the century drew to its close there were still less than 4 per cent of the population living in towns. Although by no means all of the nobility were rich, any more than they were in other east European countries, those who were lived in a state of supreme magnificence on their country estates or, far more frequently until the last quarter of the century, as absentees in Moscow or St Petersburg. Large convoys of provisions were brought by sled and by cart to these town mansions, some of which were reputedly staffed by a thousand serfs. The greatest magnates numbered their serfs in thousands; towards the end of the century Count Sheremetev owned over 180,000. Serfs were not legally slaves, although these also existed, but they were gambled away at the card-table, sold at public auction, beaten and exiled to Siberia, while their families were sometimes split up and their daughters raped by the nobility and their sons. Not all serfs were subject to such cruelties, but there must have been few who did not live in dread that they, or members of their families, might be.

57 An Englishman's rather romantic impression of the Russian village
council or *mir*, drawn in 1803.

In spite of the periodic redistribution of peasant land carried out
from the eighteenth century by the village commune, or *mir*, there
is evidence to show that there were considerable distinctions in wealth
between the serfs. Some managed to become considerable proprietors
(although the land had legally to be held in their lord's name), while a
few even became rouble-millionaire factory-owners, employing free
men even though they still remained in a state of serfdom. Many of
the state peasants on Crown estates (about two-fifths of the total
by the emancipation) were better treated and from 1788 they were
allowed to buy serfs themselves. There were also a very small number
of free peasants who had purchased their freedom or gained it
through military service. But for the vast mass of serfs on noblemen's
estates life continued to be uncertain and harsh, their only recourse
being flight, suicide or revolt. Between 1801 and the emancipation
there were nearly 1,500 separate peasant risings, some of them local,
but others widespread. In spite of all their sufferings, the peasants
retained their simple faith that the land was God's and that one day
it would be restored to them, perhaps through the intervention of
that father-figure, the tsar. This messianic belief explains the extra-
ordinary religious fervour with which the peasants supported the

58 Moscow, 10 January 1775: the rebel Pugachev and his accomplices await execution.

revolt led by Emelian Pugachev, a Don Cossack, who had proclaimed himself the true tsar, Peter III, in 1773. Many nobles were murdered and their homes burnt. In 1774, Pugachev was defeated in a battle near Tsaritsyn, not far from the spot where Stenka Razin had started his revolt. The peasants had to wait almost another century until the true tsar, Alexander II, released them from their serfdom.

In the south of Europe as a whole, economic rather than personal serfdom was the main problem. The personal serfdom that still existed was abolished mainly in the last quarter of the eighteenth century and the early years of the nineteenth. Although detailed knowledge of the changes in the south is still scanty, it appears that the necessity to feed a growing population (which may have increased in Italy, for example, from about thirteen million in 1700 to seventeen million by 1770), and more especially the increased foreign demand for luxuries like wine and raw materials for industry such as silk and oil, stimulated the growth of agriculture in traditionally progressive areas, like Lombardy, and also in some new areas. English shippers and merchants played a major part in introducing new foreign wines to the heavy-drinking upper and middle classes at home who were finding the highly taxed French wines expensive. Port was developed by English shippers from the harsh, thin wines of the Douro valley after the Treaty of Methuen (1703) had reduced duties on Portuguese wines, and other merchants introduced new wines like Sicilian marsala.

The social and economic structures of these declining countries were so fossilized in places that they scarcely admitted of any movement. Even in the most advanced regions, like Lombardy, most of the taxation fell on peasants and citizens and on trade, though Maria Theresa had some success in the middle of the century in transferring a fairer share of it to the great ecclesiastical corporations and wealthy nobility, who owned much of the land. Her son (later Leopold II), as Grand Duke of Tuscany, tried to abolish mortmain and to persuade the religious orders to convert sharecropping and short leases into hereditary leaseholds, but with only limited success. In Spain the huge estates of magnates, or grandees, were preserved by entail and increased by marriages of convenience so that, according to one eighteenth-century estimate, about one-third of all the cultivable land was held by four great houses.[35] A few of the lesser nobility and many more of the thousands of *hidalgos,* a legacy of the Reconquest, were poor, and some of the latter were reduced to begging. Banditry

59 A Spanish gentleman reduced to begging, from Goya's *Journal-Album* (1803–24).

and beggary were pandemic in the Iberian peninsula. Alentejo, a province of Portugal, was full of vagabonds and robbers in the eighteenth century, and any wedding might attract eighty or a hundred uninvited, starving guests.[36] There were few provinces where peasants were either moderately prosperous or secure: Basque, Navarra and Catalonia were some of the exceptions. But even in these extremely backward societies the sheer strength of economic forces created by the extravagance of the nobility, the ambitions of the *nouveaux riches*, the land hunger of the peasants, started to break up the fossilized structure. In Naples and Sicily the bourgeoisie and wealthier peasants, some of whom may originally have been agricultural improvers, were forced by the indifference of landlords and the difficulties of enclosures to turn into rack-renters, letting out their leased land to smaller peasants at enormous profits. It was another downward twist of the screw. A combination of social, economic and climatic factors, which had restricted progress for so many years, still appeared to present insurmountable obstacles: entail, mortmain, absentee grandees, urban *rentiers, métayage,* short leases, internal tariffs, poor communications, and above all perhaps the very high investment needed in semi-arid regions for irrigation and tree crops, prevented much change or improvement.

What had been achieved in eighteenth-century Europe? With perhaps one exception, there had been no really dramatic national transformations either in agriculture or in landholding. The rural history of each nation still flowed very much along its accustomed course, though often at a faster pace and with local diversions into different channels. But there had been a remarkable change in thinking and ideas: a much greater consciousness of the connections between agricultural progress and the structure of society as a whole, a widespread rejection of serfdom, and a greater awareness of the possibilities in commercial farming, though many years were to pass before these ideas penetrated into Russia. Agriculturally, progress had been very patchy. Much of the countryside, even in western Europe, remained so neglected and unimproved that the wolf – banished from England by the seventeenth century – and the bear were still the common enemies of cattle and sheep and, sometimes, of human beings too. Nevertheless, Europe, whose population may have increased from 105 million to 172 million during the century, seems to have been better able to feed itself. Some widespread famines continued to occur: in Sweden and Finland in 1697; in France and Sweden in

60 The taming of the countryside continued to be localized, and in some neglected areas of western Europe the bear was still a common sight in the eighteenth century.

1709; in Belgium and France in 1740–43; in Italy in 1764–66; in Sweden and Norway in 1771–73; and in Norway again in 1807–8. But the effects of a bad harvest gradually became less severe. The famine in Finland at the end of the seventeenth century is estimated to have caused the death of one-third of the population, and the effects in France in 1740 were also severe, but this was the last really disastrous old-style famine in the north of France at least, though the dearth of 1788 was to have grave political consequences.

The reasons for the increase in the population of Europe in the second half of the eighteenth century are still disputed. Was it predominantly due to agriculture? Or were there other causes? If the former, what

61 Russian peasants were driven from their homes by fears of starvation in 1891.

parts were played by improved technology, commercial farming, harder work, climatic changes, freer trade, better roads, and dietary changes to potatoes and corn? We do not have the answers to these questions. But whatever the cause, many European countries did start to escape from what appears to have been the age-old cyclic population rhythm: a poor harvest, many deaths, postponed marriages, followed by a better harvest and lower grain prices when, as one Swedish official report of 1761 commented: 'At once girls and boys were ready for the bridal bed, and for married couples love began to burn more vigorously.'[37] In the nineteenth century there were local dearths, the Irish potato famine, and widespread famine in Russia as late as 1891.[38] But even before the import of cheap wheat from the United States in the 1870s, Europe was able to sustain a rapidly rising population mainly from its own resources. The agricultural revolution had worked.

62 *The Emigrants*, by Erskine Nicol. The Irish potato famine of 1845–49, in which about a million people died, caused many more men and women to seek new opportunities in North America.

The peasantry survived into the nineteenth century, still enserfed in the east, the Balkans and a few parts of western Europe; weak in countries where the traditional landed classes remained strong, as in England, north-east and east Germany, southern Italy and much of Spain and Portugal; but more powerful in other countries, such as France, where they had obtained full legal possession of their land without being burdened by redemption payments. There had long been some peasants in western Europe who were eager to adapt to market forces, from the English yeoman to the French *fermier,* and there were others, like the Flemish peasants and the Danish freeholders, who were not loath to do so when the opportunity arose. Those who were willing or able to accept the far more rapid pace of change in the market during the nineteenth century were able to survive, but there were many others who did not have the opportunity to do so or were reluctant to abandon their centuries-old way of life and their aim of self-sufficiency. Increasingly, as the century progressed, they were to be left stranded in their isolated rural poverty outside the mainstream of modern life, or swept away entirely by the strong, swirling currents of the times.

In the nineteenth century, the population explosion had a shattering effect on peasant hopes of self-sufficiency in many parts of Europe by fragmenting even further the small and inconveniently divided farms, a legacy of partible inheritance, sub-letting, sales and the system of open-field farming. Fragmentation was greatest in regions of partible inheritance, as in much of south-west Germany, where the land was split up equally among heirs; the *Code Napoléon,* which was imposed on France and some of the conquered lands in Europe, modified the pattern slightly by allowing the testator to dispose of a certain proportion of land as he wished, enabling him to give his eldest son the largest share. To mitigate the effects of excessive pressure on available land, peasants in some parts of Europe adopted a policy of family limitation: it is possible that the relatively small

63, 64 Two aspects of modern farming: *above left*, aerial fertilization on a Scottish forestry project; *left*, a 'sweatbox' piggery for producing animals more economically.

65 Swiss herdsmen and their animals leaving to spend the summer on the upper pastures, where some common land has survived to this day.

rise in the population of France during the nineteenth century may have been the result of peasant abstention. Other peasants in western Europe exchanged land, made marriages of convenience, or bought out co-heirs; but unconsolidated small farms, sometimes split up into a hundred plots or more, have remained one of the major agricultural problems to this day, being particularly common in parts of Belgium, Germany, Austria, France, Italy and the Iberian peninsula. As late as 1960, over half of the farms in the six original members of the European Economic Community – France, West Germany, Italy, the Netherlands, Belgium and Luxembourg – were of less than twelve and a half acres. Farms were even smaller in the irrigated regions of Valencia in Spain, where almost three-quarters were under one acre in size.[1]

The gradual extinction of common rights – a subject which still awaits investigation in any detail – seems to have brought mixed benefits to the peasantry. In Sweden–Finland the enclosure of the common land began in the eighteenth century, and it proceeded more vigorously in Sweden after the enclosure law of 1803, modified in 1827. In Germany most of the commons had been divided up by the end of the nineteenth century, but the process was much slower in many parts of southern Europe, where common pastures still exist in some woodlands, Alpine valleys and the mountainous areas of the Iberian peninsula. Although some smallholdings were often created when the commons were enclosed, many younger sons in regions of primogeniture were robbed of cottar rights, adding to the total of the landless. In all countries the problem of the landless had existed for many years, but it was exacerbated in the nineteenth century by the growth of population.

This relative over-population developed at a time when, one by one, the myriad threads which had bound together town and countryside were being snapped and broken, depriving the poor peasant and members of his family of chances to supplement their income by working part-time at some industrial activity, which, with common rights, had long been one of the major props of the peasant economy. Rural manufacturing of consumer goods, from clogs to cuckoo clocks, did not disappear overnight. Throughout the nineteenth

66 'Making clogs', from Diderot's *Encyclopédie* (1762). Small rural industries still survive in some remote areas, but many country crafts died out during the nineteenth century as the population became increasingly concentrated in industrial towns.

century it still retained some importance in England – and even more elsewhere – with a continuing demand for such country products as rush and osier baskets, mats and chair seats, wooden bowls, toys and spoons, and also for imported goods such as bast mats from Russia and rugs and tapestries from the Balkans. Indeed, in many of the remoter parts of Europe, country people have continued to make such goods to this day, setting up their stalls at regular markets in the woods, as they do in Poland, for example, though nowadays the toys they sell are as likely to be made of plastic as of natural materials.

The process of shifting heavy industry to the towns was equally slow, extending over a period of a century or more, and culminating in thirty or so years of intense activity and great expansion – W. W. Rostow's 'take-off' period. This occurred at the end of the eighteenth century in England, but later in France, from 1830 to 1860, and in Germany, from 1850 to 1873, being delayed by a number of factors, including the long wars of the eighteenth century and internal customs barriers and tolls.[2] Spinning and weaving, which had kept so many peasant families above the destitution line, were gradually transferred from the home to the workshop and the factory. In eighteenth-century England, those peasants who combined small-scale farming with hand-loom weaving in Lancashire and other parts of the north had been the aristocrats of the working classes, with

67 Wilhelm Leibl, *The Spinning Wheel* (1892). When spinning and weaving moved into the factories, the peasantry lost yet another source of income.

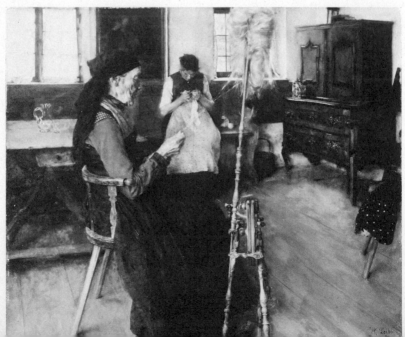

68 Paul Sandby, *The Iron Forge between Dolgelli and Barmouth in Merioneth Shire* (1776). The shifting of heavy industry from the countryside helped to create a serious social imbalance between town and country.

their high boots and ruffed shirts and often a £5 Bank of England note tucked into their hatband as an overt badge of affluence. But after the development of a successful power-loom, originally patented by the Reverend Edmund Cartwright in 1785, they were slowly reduced, according to one official report published in 1827, to the last stages of disease and want, too proud or too weak to venture from their isolated homes and hamlets to seek parish relief. Spinning had started to disappear from the home into the factory earlier, and straw-plaiting and glove-making went the same way later.

Another development which had disastrous effects for many peasants was the rapid expansion of the synthetic dye industry, mainly in Germany, after the British chemist Sir William Perkin had succeeded in making mauve from coal-tar in 1856. The cultivation and preparation of vegetable dyes had formerly provided a profitable and most suitable activity for small-scale farmers. Garancine, a red dyestuff, was prepared from madder root by boiling it in acidulated water; woad was cultivated for blue dye and weld for yellow. In southern Europe peasants collected kermes, the pregnant aphides infesting the evergreen oak, which provide a brilliant scarlet dye when dried. These extremely ancient activities and skills became increasingly unnecessary.

In the same way, there was a fall in demand for barilla, an impure alkali made mainly in Spain and Sicily by burning the cultivated plant *Salsola soda*, after new chemical processes were introduced in the glass and soap manufacturing industries; and for the same reason the kelp (burnt seaweed) industry on the west coast of Scotland and the north-west coast of France started to decline. Colza oil, extracted from rape-seed, lost its importance as an illuminant after kerosene started to be used in oil-lamps from the 1860s, although it continued to be used in other industrial processes. (Rape and cole-seed remained important farm crops, being prized as fodder for their greenstuff and oil cake – the residue after the seeds had been crushed.) But the most important divorce between industry and the country-side was caused by the wider use of the coke-smelting process for making iron; this created the often concentrated trinity of coal, iron and engineering towns, in place of the diffusion of industry in the wooded countryside with the charcoal-burner, the ironmaster, the travelling millwright and the agricultural toolmaker exercising their skills in metal and in wood, particularly with the timber of the hornbeam from which so many early cogs and screws were made.

Most towns had also once possessed many direct and intimate links with agriculture, not only in their markets and their fairs and through the system of *métayage*, but also in the contiguity of field and city wall and the existence of dairying in the alleys of the cities themselves. As late as 1866, in London alone, cowkeepers still had over 9,500 milking cows in stalls at the rear of their town dairies; but over half of these were killed in the serious outbreak of rinderpest in that year. As a result, stricter sanitary regulations were imposed and practically all of the town dairies in London were closed within a few years.[3]

For many centuries towns had been one of the main stimulants of agricultural activity both in the immediate vicinity and in more distant regions. They had caused market-gardens and orchards to flourish near by; they had brought about an increase in overseas trade – grain from the Baltic through the Sound, sugar from the West Indies – and they had also increased overland trade, particularly in livestock, the only farm produce which provides its own means of transport, so that even by the end of the fifteenth century market ordinances in Cologne mention sales of cattle from Denmark, Poland and Hungary. Even so, international trade in farm produce remained relatively small until the nineteenth century when towns of a different size and kind were being created.

In England, where modern industrial centres first developed, towns such as Manchester, Liverpool, Birmingham, Hull and Sheffield were expanding in the middle of the eighteenth century, though probably none had a population of more than 50,000: the capital, with its estimated population of 650,000, remained an exception. A century later, London, with its population of 2,685,000, still remained exceptional, but Manchester had 303,000 residents, Liverpool 376,000, and Sheffield 135,000. By 1851 the majority of the population in England and Wales were living in towns and cities for the first time in history.

69, 70 Many intimate links between town and country survived well into the nineteenth century. *Left*, 'Who will buy my young ducklings?' (Göttingen); *right*, milk-seller in the streets of London.

Wil ji junge Dübecken koepen

Although there were large capital cities and a few other big towns in the rest of Europe, and some early exceptional areas such as the province of Holland in the Netherlands, the process of urbanization was generally much slower. The majority of the German population were living in towns before 1900, but that point was not reached in France until 1930 or in Sweden until after the Second World War.[4] These new industrial towns were gradually to bring about a dramatic change in agriculture, by increasing the market for food to a hitherto unknown extent; by providing new means whereby these demands could be satisfied through the use of by-products from their own activities and the invention of machines and new techniques; and by developing improved means of transport which allowed farm produce to be obtained in large quantities not only from distant farms but also, increasingly, from overseas.

In the 1840s chemists in three European countries – Sir John Benet Lawes (1814–1900) in England, Justus von Liebig (1803–73) in Germany, and Jean-Baptiste Boussingault (1802–87) in France – were independently investigating the principles of artificial fertilizers. In 1843, Lawes started to manufacture superphosphates at his factory at Deptford, a revolutionary innovation which freed farmers for the first time from total dependence on natural manures. Sulphate of ammonia, originally a by-product of gasworks though now produced largely by direct synthesis, started to appear on the market a few years later with the increasing use of gas as an illuminant in the towns. Basic slag, rich in lime, a by-product of the steel-manufacturing industry, became available following the introduction of the Gilchrist-Thomas method in 1878–79. Used with discretion, these fertilizers helped to double crop yields on some farms, benefited graziers by providing better pastures, and also allowed wastelands to be taken into cultivation. Alentejo had long been one of the poorest provinces of Portugal, a large plateau of scrub and sharecroppers, overrun by sheep, goats and beggars; but towards the end of the nineteenth century much of it was cleared by large farmers and commercial companies and transformed into the country's main granary by the application of the new fertilizers.

Agricultural machines began to appear in increasing numbers and varieties from about the middle of the century. Interest had been stimulated in England by the Great Exhibition of 1851, especially by the exhibits from the United States. The small size of farms and lack of capital prevented most European farmers from taking advantage of

71 Burgess and Key's American reaper. New agricultural machines, designed for more extensive American farms, were gradually introduced by progressive English farmers in the second half of the nineteenth century.

the new machines; they were introduced gradually on large progressive farms, particularly in England. Threshing had been one of the first farm operations to be mechanized in England, initially by hand-operated machines invented by a Scottish millwright, Andrew Meikle (1719–1811), in 1784, and then by machines driven by horse- or water power and later by steam. Chaff-cutters, root-slicers and crushers followed; these, too, were operated by hand at first and then on larger farms by steam-power. Horse-drawn drills for sowing seeds in rows, advocated by Jethro Tull almost a century before, also began to be used on some farms. Although the Reverend Patrick Bell (1799–1869), a Scottish minister, had invented a practical horse-drawn reaping machine in 1828, such machines gained little favour on English farms until more efficient American reapers were displayed at the Great Exhibition in London. By 1871 about a quarter of the grain acreage on English farms was being cut mechanically, but only a very small proportion elsewhere in Europe. Even in England, however, machinery meant little more to many farmers at the end of the century than the hiring of a steam-operated threshing machine, which was more economical than employing farm workers on laborious and exhausting work with the flail.

72, 73 *Above* Steam-driven farm machines from Samuel Copland's *Agriculture Ancient and Modern* (1866). *Below* The first farm machine ever seen by many Victorian country-dwellers was the hired, steam-operated thresher.

Britain led the world in the ultimately abortive attempt to use steam-power for tilling. Numerous experiments with traction, rotary and cable-drawn ploughs were made in the 1830s and 1840s. During the 1860s cable-drawn steam-ploughs started to be used on some of the larger English farms, and they were also used later in the century on both large and medium-sized farms in Germany and Austria. The development of a tractor, powered by an internal-combustion engine, in the United States in 1889, signalled the beginning of the end for steam. Henry Ford (1863–1947) started making his highly successful tractors in 1915 and set up many overseas factories in the 1920s. But the introduction of tractors into European farming was slow. There were still 640,000 farm horses at work on English farms at the beginning of the Second World War compared with about 100,000 tractors. (The farm horse has now virtually disappeared from English farms, where there are more tractors than farm workers, although with the current high price of oil, some farmers are seriously considering re-introducing it.) Mechanization proceeded much more slowly on many of the small peasant farms of the mainland, where the grain was reaped with the sickle and the light, straight-shafted continental scythe and the main traction-power was provided by the horse, the ox, and the water-buffalo, as it still is in some remote regions to the present day.

Railways had the most dramatic consequences for agriculture. Britain started to build a railway network from the 1830s; Germany followed rapidly after the establishment of the Zollverein in 1834, the first line being built in Bavaria in the following year; France started to develop an extensive system during the Second Empire; while the small country of Belgium became the first to complete the main outline of its cross-shaped system, intersecting at Malines, in 1843. Railways provided easier access to both national and international markets, thus helping to lower prices and to abolish the spectre of local famine except in the most isolated regions; they made it easier for new machinery and new ideas to be introduced into remoter regions, and encouraged enclosures and the buying up of land to create commercially viable farms; and they allowed more cheap migrant labour to be brought in for the harvests from foreign countries. It was, however, the building of railways in other countries which had such a devastating impact on grain-growing, traditionally the primary sector of agriculture in much of western Europe. The building of railroads across the great plains of the United States

74 The Great Western Railway near Bath. The development of railways helped to reduce both the price of food and the possibility of local dearth.

and Canada (the coasts were linked in 1869 and 1885 respectively) allowed huge quantities of cheap grain, harvested from the virgin lands by mechanical reapers, to be transported to ports for shipment to Europe, while the railway 'mania' in Russia in the 1870s and 1880s greatly increased grain shipments from Baltic and Black Sea ports. At the same time the development of the improved compound engine by Alfred Holt in 1864 allowed steamships to carry bigger cargoes more economically over longer distances, so that foreign wheat could be sold more cheaply in Europe than the domestic produce. Livestock farmers also had to face new competition from overseas. Cheap canned meat started to be imported from the United States and from Australia in the 1870s, while in 1880 the first shipment of Australian frozen meat arrived in Britain in the steamship *Strathleven*, the first steamship with a refrigerated hold.

These improvements in transport occurred at a particularly bad time for many farmers in western Europe. Harvests were poor in 1877, 1878 and 1879, the last being particularly disastrous. Phylloxera, a North American aphis brought into Europe on imported vines between 1858 and 1863, brought devastation to the vineyards of

75 Poor harvests in the late 1870s, together with improved overseas transport, contributed to the agricultural depression in Europe. Farm workers organized marches to appeal for support and funds, carrying banners like the one shown here.

France where nearly two and a half million acres had been destroyed by 1885, with the result that a large part of the Charente region had to be turned over from viticulture to dairy farming. Vineyards in Germany were less seriously affected because of stricter quarantine. There were also epidemics of cattle plague, with widespread rinderpest occurring in Britain in 1877, the last major notified outbreak of the disease in that country.

The agricultural depression, which lasted until 1896 in grain prices, marked a great turning-point for the whole of agriculture in western Europe. Farmers had to become more efficient or to be shielded from the full effects of overseas competition by tariff walls. The reaction of individual countries was largely determined by their socio-economic structures. Britain, the first industrialized country in Europe, needed cheap food for its factory workers and free markets for its manufactured goods. Under pressure from the manufacturing classes, organized by Cobden in the Anti-Corn-Law League, it had repealed the Corn Law in 1846. Even though the full effects of repeal were delayed by the Crimean War in Russia and the Civil War in the United States, Britain remained faithful to its free trade principles, of which it was the leading advocate, preferring cheap food for the towns to protection of its farmers. Denmark and the Netherlands also remained free traders, for different reasons. With their minimal industrialization – the Netherlands produced no iron or steel until the First World War – they remained heavily dependent on their efficient, market-orientated peasant farmers. But practically all other countries in western Europe introduced protective tariffs for agriculture.

Bismarck set a lead in 1879. German industrialists, hard hit by the trade depression of 1873, had been agitating for more protection for several years. Until 1877, the Junkers had supported free trade, depending on grain exports to support their heavily mortgaged estates and to stave off their often-threatened bankruptcy. When exports of cheaper grain captured much of the market in England, and imports from the United States, Russia and Hungary started to depress prices on the home market, too, they also came out for protection. Bismarck, needing bigger Reich revenues to pay for defence, accepted this new alliance of iron and rye, and tariffs were introduced on some manufactured goods, grain and other farm produce in 1879. It was a fateful realignment of policy which enabled the feudal elements beyond the Elbe to survive for many more years as an economically protected group with an entrenched position in the state and in society. 'There

76 *Punch*'s Monument
to Peel' for
the repeal of
the Corn Law
in 1846.

are few historical events to which an equally disastrous effect on the
destinies of German democracy can be ascribed,' says Alexander
Gerschenkron. 'At every stage of their development in the Hohenzollern monarchy as well as in the Weimar Republic the forces of
democracy were hamstrung by the opposition of the East Elbian
aristocracy.'[5]

The German duties on grain were trebled in 1885 and increased
again two years later, when France, Italy and Belgium also introduced
agricultural duties, while Switzerland followed four years later.
In the major countries the tariffs were mainly designed, as in Germany,
to protect the big, grain-growing farmers and landowners who still
exercised great political and social power. In France the campaign for
protection was led by the aristocratic *Société des Agriculteurs de France*,
and in Italy by the big grain producers.[6]

133

What of the peasants? How did they react and fare? For them, too, this was a great turning-point. Protection was of little benefit to the peasants, except perhaps in Belgium and in Switzerland, where livestock was protected and grains were left practically free. In the larger countries – Germany, France, Italy – the duties may well have actually harmed many peasants by keeping the price of bread artificially high and thus reducing urban demand for other produce, and by making the cost of feeding-stuffs higher than it need have been. Furthermore, the tariff war between France and Italy, which lasted from 1887 to the end of the century, adversely affected many peasants, particularly in Italy, by making it more difficult for them to export. The general trends in agriculture were moving far more swiftly against traditional peasant farming. The capitalist farmer or large leaseholder had great advantages in credit, mechanization, marketing and sometimes cheap labour, which the peasant producing for the market did not share.

There had always been two powerful and conflicting traditions in the peasant world, that of self-protection and that of co-operation: the former led to enclosures and the jealous preservation of individual or family rights, and the latter to the appointment of the communal shepherd and herdsman in the wastelands and to mutual aid in the grain harvest and in the vintage. As in former times of adversity and of rising population, peasants in many west European countries banded together, often under the gentle persuasion of their superiors, to form co-operatives, which have remained the main basis of surviving peasant prosperity to this day. In many western European countries, supply co-operatives now buy a wide range of farming necessities such as fertilizers, seeds, fodder and machinery at lower prices than individual peasants could obtain; marketing and processing co-operatives collect produce from the farm, grade, sort and process it, and find new markets where they sell in bulk; and credit co-operatives and banks provide short-term loans in temporary financial difficulties and longer-term loans for restocking farms and for making improvements to them.

Although the fundamental nature of these co-operatives is everywhere the same, nationally they reflect the social structure of their respective countries. The most successful advances in co-operation occurred in Denmark, where the ground had been prepared by the agrarian reforms, autocratically imposed towards the end of the eighteenth century, which had created a large class of secure peasant

77 A co-operative dairy established in a former rural deanery on the island of Møn, Denmark, c. 1889.

owners on consolidated farms preserved from fragmentation by a law of 1819. Danish farmers had a wider outlook than most other peasants in Europe as a result of the introduction of compulsory elementary education in 1814 – patchy, inadequate and part-time though it continued to be for a further century – and of the famous folk schools created in the 1840s by Bishop Grundtvig (1783–1872), an evangelical romantic: 'We are educated to be critics instead of creators. . . . The eternal criticising will exhaust our human life-force.'[7] With the advent of the agricultural depression, Denmark changed the emphasis of its farming from exporting grain to exporting livestock and dairy produce. It became a huge processing plant, converting cheap American grain into bacon and eggs for the breakfast-table of the English middle classes, and it also exported considerable quantities of butter and livestock. Co-operative dairies were established, the first in 1882, to make butter in bulk with the centrifugal separator invented by a Swede, Gustav de Laval (1845–1913), in place of the centuries-old butter-churn. The great extension of co-operation laid the foundations for new prosperity as an agricultural exporting nation in the twentieth century, with farm labourers also benefiting after the passing of the Smallholdings Act of 1899, which gave state mortgages to those who could raise the initial deposit of 10 per cent to buy a plot of land.

In the Netherlands, too, the co-operative movement flourished, even though many peasants were tenants rather than owners. The first supply co-op was set up in 1877 to buy fertilizers, and ten years later the first of the unique auction societies was formed, where market-gardeners can sell their produce at time-saving Dutch auctions in which the price descends rapidly from a high level instead of increasing slowly from an initial bid. Many other co-operatives were formed in the Netherlands, including the first credit bank in 1896, although owing to the operation of *verzuiling* (pillarization), which divided the country into three main groups of Catholic, Protestant and 'neutral', there was some wasteful triplication, with, for example, separate goat-breeders' associations for Catholics and for Protestants. In the northern part of Belgium the *Boerenbond*, established by a Catholic priest in 1887, helped to sustain religious faith by earthly co-operation in the devout, Flemish- or Dutch-speaking part of this small country, which is still so bitterly divided along linguistic lines.

Many French peasants clung much longer to their traditional way of life, with collective grazing on the stubble persisting in parts of Beauce and Picardy into the present century, but even in France local co-operatives gradually gained some hold. Co-operative dairies were set up first in the former areas of viticulture following the disastrous attacks of phylloxera; cereal co-operatives were formed in the south of France after the slump in wine prices in the 1930s; and wine-growing co-operatives were also established, which now market about 40 per cent of all the wine produced. One of the most important co-operative ventures originated in Germany where Friedrich Raiffeisen (1818–88) established a loan society for peasants in the Rhineland in 1849, followed by a co-operative bank in 1862, which became a model for those set up in many other European countries later. It is an interesting reflection of the very different balance between town and country, peasants and factory workers, that there were few agricultural co-operatives in England, but that the first consumers' co-operative was formed by a group of weavers in Rochdale, Lancashire, in 1844.

Only a minority of the European peasantry benefited initially through such schemes. Other peasants and younger sons who could not gain a living on their native soil migrated in their thousands, as seasonal workers to larger farms or estates in other parts of their country or to foreign lands where there was some demand for their labour. In Italy peasants moved from the south to the rice-fields of Lombardy in the north; in Portugal from the north to the grain-fields of Alentejo. Irish mowers crossed the sea to help in the English grain harvest, while others went to the Lowlands of Scotland at a later season to assist in the lifting of the potato crop. The Junker estates in Germany attracted thousands of migrant workers from Poland, Galicia and Hungary; by 1914 about half a million foreign workers were employed in German agriculture every year. Through-out the century, as the population grew, transport improved, and the final abolition of serfdom gave freedom of movement, there developed a massive seasonal migration of agricultural workers (whose detailed history still needs to be written) from the east of Europe to the west, from grain-fields to vineyards, from highlands to lowlands. Many other peasants migrated to the towns, particularly towards the end of the century, and some of them, disillusioned by their experiences there, may later have helped to increase the number of emigrants to more hopeful lands across the seas.

The trickle of emigrants at the beginning of the nineteenth century to the New World, Latin America and the 'white' countries in the British Empire had become a flood by the end. In Britain, farm labourers and workers were encouraged to emigrate by the govern-ment and by charitable organizations in the period of unemployment following the Napoleonic Wars. 'When the population of a country increases beyond the demand for labour, the Unemployed Poor must either be supported by alms, or support themselves by pillage,' wrote one well-meaning pamphleteer. 'The natural relief of this condition is the emigration of the unemployed.'[8] In Norway, where the population growth after the Napoleonic Wars rivalled that in Ireland, there was a massive increase in landless labourers and poor cottagers. Although the first party of fifty-two emigrants, who left Stavanger for New York on 5 July 1825, departed mainly for religious reasons, the motivation of thousands more who left later in the century was mainly economic.

The first really big wave of immigrants to engulf the United States in the nineteenth century came after outbreaks of potato blight, a fungus which left the tubers an uneatable pulp, black and rotting in the ground, had occurred in many parts of Europe between 1845 and 1849. The effects were worst in Ireland, where the majority of peasants were dependent on the potato for subsistence. An estimated one million people died, either through starvation or through typhus or fever, and a further 800,000 or more emigrated, mainly to the United States, over a period of five years. The potato famine also increased emigration from south-west Germany to the United States and from Scotland to Canada. Emigration from Europe continued at an increasing pace, with sudden peaks and surges. Between 1852 and 1892 emigration to the United States from Germany alone exceeded 100,000 annually in eighteen separate years.[9] The agricultural depression increased the total. About 300,000 people left Denmark, mainly for the United States, between 1870 and 1914, and there was an even bigger exodus from other Scandinavian countries. An increasing number of Spaniards and Portuguese left their countries, sailing along what was by then a centuries-old migratory route to South America. But it was the exodus from Italy which, after that from Ireland, has justly attracted most attention.

Ever since the end of the Napoleonic Wars, Italians mainly from the north had been migrating temporarily or permanently to other European countries and to Latin America. An increasing number left in the 1870s, still mainly for other European countries and for South America, but from the 1880s the total was greatly swollen by peasants from the south, and by the end of the century the United States had become the main magnet. There, living in squalid tenements and exploited by *padroni*, fellow-countrymen who took an excessive share of their wages, they worked on the New York subway, on railroads and building sites and in coal-mines, hoping to create, as so many of them did, a new life for the second or the third generation; others returned later as *Americani* to their native villages, wealthy enough to set up as shopkeepers or smallholders. This outflow into the New World swept along with it a few germs from the old. The Mafia had originally been encouraged to murder and to set up its clandestine groups of a dozen or so men by Sicilian landowners who employed them to protect their crops and livestock against bandits. It had already become a law unto itself in its native Sicily, where it terrorized its employers and extracted tributes from them, before a few of its members emigrated to the United States to put their talents to new uses.

78 It is hard to believe that these shacks in a New York tenement yard represented an improvement on conditions in Europe; yet from these beginnings many emigrants were able to create a new and better life for the second or third generations.

Even these massive outflows did little to drain the pool of the land-less and the poor in Europe: for one peasant who left there were many more who remained. It is estimated that 'between 1880 and 1915 emigration removed every year from the population of Italy something like 3–4 persons in every thousand'.[10] Evictions and rack-renting continued to occur as they had done for many centuries, particularly on the fringes of western Europe. In Scotland at the beginning of the nineteenth century many thousands of crofters, whose families had sometimes been tenants of the same land for four centuries, were dispossessed in the Highland clearances to make way for sheep and deer, and evictions went on in Ireland throughout the century. Where he could, the peasant fought back with his traditional weapons of fire, club and knife and, in Ireland from 1880, with a new non-violent weapon – the boycott – which originated in County Mayo when peasants refused to work for Captain Charles Cunning-ham Boycott (1832–97), a land agent who had carried out evictions on the estate he administered. Although the Irish situation with its general depression of the peasants into a far more homogeneous

79 Van Gogh's *Potato Eaters* (1885), desperately poor but attached to the land and to their old dreams – the social problem that would not go away.

group and its other focal points encouraged rebellion, it was never easy for the European peasantry as a whole to sustain revolt; they were too isolated, too attached to their land, their livestock and their crops, and usually too much in conflict and competition with other peasants. Moreover, their stubborn attachment to the land – the keystone of their whole existence – gave them the opportunity to retreat temporarily or permanently into a minimal subsistence, as so many of them did in this age of change. Their small plots enabled them to survive for many more years, increasingly poor in relative terms – Van Gogh's *Potato Eaters* – and more and more anachronistic in the new era of industry and the growing market: the social problem that would not go away. They remained conservative in a deep and fundamental sense, harbouring values, attitudes and desires which were not of the urban age, too large a group to be completely ignored and too unknown to be understood – a canker in the body social and politic, which extremists of both left and right later sought to exploit for their own purposes, though both the communists and the Nazis mistrusted and basically disliked the peasantry.

During the nineteenth century intellectuals from the towns went out into the countryside of western Europe seeking adherents for their causes among the peasantry and evidence to justify their preconceived notions about them. The liberals had some success in Denmark and Switzerland; the revolutionary republicans in the Young Ireland movement, like John Mitchel (1815–75), failed disastrously when they tried to incite the starving peasants to rebel in the middle of the famine; and the Italian socialists had the biggest success in penetrating the countryside after they had helped to organize strikes among landless labourers in the Po valley in the 1880s. But even in Italy the conflict of interests between landless labourers, sharecroppers and peasant proprietors restricted success. The historic divisions of wealth and interests prevented the formation of a united socio-economic class, and peasant suspicions of the town made political alignments uneasy. Scandinavia, with its long-established tradition of the independent odal freeholder, which persisted as myth even when it had little accord with reality, was the main exception in western Europe. Strong agrarian parties arose there in the nineteenth century, which have been replaced in modern times by agrarian parties of the centre in Norway and in Sweden, and by liberal democrats and a more radical liberal party (a coalition of small peasants, urban intellectuals and professional men) in Denmark. There is also a reasonably large peasants' party in Switzerland. Elsewhere in western Europe, however, peasants have tended to make their voices heard through the main political parties, generally, with the chief exceptions of Italian and some French peasants, through parties of the right.

Nationalists were also active in the countryside during the nineteenth century, transcribing folk-songs and tales and collecting costumes to sustain their belief that the peasants were the preservers of the precious heritage of patriotic virtues, the missing link between the glories of the Middle Ages and the burgeoning national revival of modern times, whose folk consciousness was embodied in their crafts and their arts. The reverence for folk art was strongest in those countries which were themselves divided or dominated by some foreign power, but, as Robert Wildhaber has recently pointed out, the 'concept of folk art as an expression of nationalism, is itself a piece of nineteenth-century folklore'.[11]

This nationalistic passion was taken to a new extreme of racism by the National Socialists in the present century, with their slogan of

4.REICHSBAUERNTAG
22.-29.NOV. GOSLAR 1936

80 'Fourth Imperial Peasants' Congress': it is easy to understand the appeal, for the peasants, of a political party which appeared to take their problems seriously at last.

'blood and soil' (*Blut und Boden*). Originally, the National Socialists had had few connections with the German peasantry, but their promise of 'relief from the burdens of debt, taxation and falling prices'[12] struck a responsive chord among the indebted peasants, struggling to gain a bare living from their small, divided plots, who had been temporarily relieved of some of their indebtedness by the inflation after the First World War but were thrown into a panic by the depression of 1928. There was already a strong agrarian movement, particularly well organized in Schleswig-Holstein, where Hitler gained his first rural support in 1928 by capturing 4 per cent of the vote, which, with the worsening agricultural crisis, increased to 27 per cent by 1930. 'Schleswig-Holstein', writes Karl Dietrich Bracher, 'became a milestone on the NSDAP's forward march towards a popular mass party.'[13] The National Socialists also gained early successes in Lower Saxony and after 1929 in most other rural areas. The German peasants saw in Hitler the means of their own salvation. For the second time in half a century, the failure to achieve a just solution to the agricultural problem, which was partly a result of Bismarck's policy of 1879, was to cast the whole of Germany into an even deeper dungeon of anti-democratic doom.

Soon after Hitler came to power he paid off his debts to the peasants – in words if not always in deeds – by passing the Farm Inheritance Act of 1933, which was designed to freeze the farm structure by making peasant holdings indivisible and inalienable. The preamble to the Act said: 'The German Government intends to preserve the German peasants' holdings as the source of the life-blood of the German nation by safeguarding ancient German customs of succession. Peasants' holdings are to be protected against indebtedness and partition among the heirs, to the end that they may always be held by free peasants as a family heritage.'[14] Only Aryans who were technically competent and politically reliable were allowed to own farms. But reality was different from Hitler's promises. Although imports of agricultural produce were reduced and subsidies gave farmers higher and more assured incomes, the gap between living standards in the towns and in the country continued to increase and the flight from the land went on. And who can doubt that, if the Third Reich had survived for even a minute proportion of its planned thousand years, the rigid control of the peasant from above by the Reich Food Estate would have produced, not only in Germany but also in settled and subject lands, what Doreen Warriner was already predicting in 1939 – 'a new kind of serfdom'?[15]

In Russia, the peasant problem (as it was always called, in contrast to the 'land question' in western Europe) proved to be even more intractable. Until 1861, serfdom, with all its evil consequences for the whole of society, was still an integral part of the backward Russian state: there were far fewer towns in the vast Russian countryside to stimulate agricultural improvement. The peasants still lived in their messianic dream that the land would one day be theirs. Sporadic uprisings and revolts against their masters continued to occur; no less than 144 landowners were murdered by serfs between 1835 and 1854. Towards the middle of the century rumours swept through different parts of the countryside that freedom could be gained by working on the railroads, that the Crimea would be resettled by free men, that the French emperor would make emancipation of the Russian serfs a condition for granting peace at the conclusion of the Crimean War; but peasants who fled from their masters' estates in search of these mirages were brought back, cowed and beaten, under armed guards.

The protests of the peasants against the backward, autocratic nature of society were now supported by some isolated, but culturally influential, voices of nobles and intellectuals. The open attack on serfdom and autocracy made by Alexander Radischev (1749–1802) in his *Journey from St Petersburg to Moscow* created a political and literary sensation when it was published in 1790: he was sentenced to death, commuted later to exile in Siberia, where he was freed in 1801, a sick and broken man, who committed suicide in the following year. Other attacks on the state were circulated among intellectuals in hand-written manuscripts, like the second part of *In the Village*, which was written by Alexander Pushkin (1799–1837) in 1818, but was not openly published until after the Emancipation. One of the most implacable opponents of serfdom was Ivan Turgenev (1818–83), whose mother had exiled two of her serfs to Siberia because they failed to bow as she passed;[16] many of his stories obliquely attacking serfdom escaped the censor's hand, though he too, like Pushkin, was banished to the family estate for a time. The socialist Alexander Herzen (1812–70) went into voluntary exile in London so that he could be free to attack what he called *Baptised Property* (1853), and four years later to publish his periodical *The Bell,* which was officially banned in Russia but achieved such renown that it was sold openly and was reputed to be read by the tsar himself. But these were lonely voices, and the mass of landowners remained opposed to emancipation. The distance and the difference between lord and master was still so great that Leo Tolstoy (1828–1910), full of youthful idealism, was forced to give up his attempts to carry out reforms on his family's estates at Yasnaya Polyana, south of Moscow, in the face of his serfs' mistrust and suspicions. Alliances between intellectuals and peasants, as we have seen, have usually been short-lived and uneasy.

Serfdom imprisoned not only the peasants but all members of society in its backwardness. Landowners, with some few exceptions,[17] were reluctant to improve the management of their estates while they still had such large forces of cheap labour. Even the tsars, powerful though they were, were trapped in a political dilemma, fearful that emancipation might alienate the noble support on which their own autocracy depended, but conscious that the continuance of serfdom could only increase unrest among the peasants. During the first half of the nineteenth century, the tsars introduced some small measures of reform, though many of them were evaded or ignored. Labour services were prohibited on Sundays; the sale of serfs without land was banned; and newspapers were prohibited from advertising public auctions of serfs. Under Alexander I (1777–1825) there was even a limited emancipation of the serfs in the Baltic provinces of Estonia, Courland and Livonia between 1816 and 1819, but as they were freed without land, unrest continued in those provinces. Secret committee after secret committee examined the peasant problem in the reign of Nicholas I (1796–1855), but it was defeat in the Crimean War which convinced the new tsar, Alexander II (1818–81), that the serfs must be emancipated. As in Prussia, fifty years before, it was foreign generals – grossly incompetent though many of them were – who eventually drove home the lesson of even greater Russian inefficiency. A few days after the end of the war, Alexander told representatives of the Moscow nobility: 'It is better to begin to destroy serfdom from above, than to wait until that time when it begins to destroy itself from below.'[18] After much consultation and discussion the law freeing the serfs, over half of the peasant population of forty-one and a half million, was signed by the tsar on 19 February 1861, and published early in the following months.

The law, which is generally considered to be one of the classic turning-points in European history, was exceedingly complex.[19] Although it gave the serfs much more than the peasants in the Baltic provinces had been granted forty years before, it was unfairly weighted in favour of the nobility and failed to satisfy the serfs; revolts which broke out in several places immediately after the law was published were followed by others in different places during the next three or four years. The serfs obtained neither complete freedom nor the amount of land they had hoped for, as the landowners retained one-third to one-half of their estates. Household serfs did not gain their freedom (without land) for two years and all other serfs had to stay on their holdings for a further nine years, after which they were allowed to leave under certain conditions. Most peasants were placed under the authority of the *mir,* the self-governing village commune, which held the title-deeds to their land, issued internal passports, and was communally responsible for all taxes. There were also special peasant courts, which retained the right of corporal punishment even though it had been abolished in other courts. Allotments of land also failed to satisfy the peasants; the land was split up into scattered strips and regularly redistributed by the *mir,* as it had been before the Emancipation, in accordance with the needs created by the changing composition of each family. Many peasants, particularly in the fertile black earth region, were cheated out of their fair share by landowners and officials; and all of them, unless they opted to take a smallholding, which was only one-quarter of the size of the maximum allotment allowed by law, had to pay redemption charges for forty-nine years in addition to heavy taxes. State peasants, who by then totalled nearly nineteen million men and women, fared much better when they were freed a few years later, retaining all their land and generally making smaller redemption payments. Most peasants felt cheated by the results of their long-delayed emancipation, which left a mass of unfulfilled hopes, un-realized dreams and huge areas of gross inefficiency which continued to trouble successive Russian governments for many years.

The peasantry, which still constituted the vast majority of the Russian population, could not be omitted from any calculations concerning social advance. The populists, influenced by the ideas of the anarchist Mikhail Bakunin (1814–76) and of Alexander Herzen, based their hopes of revolution upon the countryside. They believed that Russia could go direct from a peasant to a socialist state without passing through the intermediate stage of capitalism. This faith was engendered by the Russian *mir,* which redistributed village land among the peasants. Did not this, they believed, represent an historic tradition of Slavic communism upon which a socialist state might be based? The controversy over the origins and nature of the *mir* split the intellectual world of Russia in the second half of the nineteenth century. While populists, anarchists and Slavophiles saw in it a unique hope of Russian salvation, the westerners, who drew their inspiration from the rapid progress in the other half of Europe, claimed that the *mir* was nothing but a recent creation of the state to ensure that each peasant family owned enough land to pay its taxes.

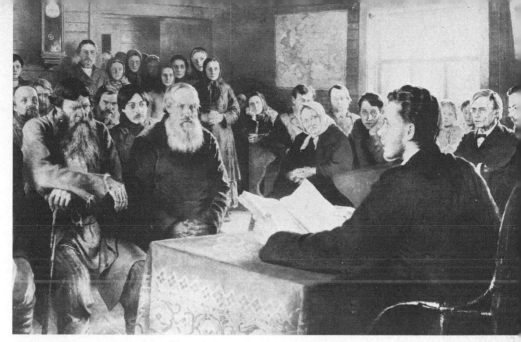

81 A student agitator spreading the message of revolution among the Russian peasantry in 1905.

We do not need to follow all the labyrinthine twists and turns in this debate: the true answer still remains somewhat elusive. But the populists were no more successful in gaining support for their abstract views in the countryside than members of the Young Ireland movement had been among the Irish peasantry. During the 1870s young Russian men and women – mainly students – dressed up in peasant clothes and went out from the towns to spread their revolutionary message among the country people and to purify themselves in the springs of their Slavic faith. 'The short period of our stay among the people revealed to us all that was doctrinaire and "literary" in our aspirations,' said one Russian revolutionary in 1881.[20]

Although the anarchists came the nearest of all revolutionaries to offering the peasants what they most desired, they gained relatively little support in either eastern or western Europe. In France, Pierre-Joseph Proudhon (1809–65), an anarchist of peasant stock, gained no more support than had the populists in Russia with his schemes for a France freed from the toils of large-scale competition in banking, speculation and industry, with three-quarters of the anticipated population of fifty-three and a half million living comfortably on

147

their twelve-and-a-half-acre plots and still having a surplus to support another thirteen and a half million industrial workers, public servants and soldiers. Princes fared no better. The schemes of mutual aid formulated by Prince Peter Kropotkin (1842–1921), the Russian anarchist, made no significant impact on peasants. Even those peasants who could read were usually less interested in intellectual abstractions than in the possession of the land, which they, as the oldest surviving social group in Europe, felt rightfully to be theirs. They could not be slotted easily into any modern socio-economic analysis.

Marx was very conscious of this ambiguity in the peasants' status. In a celebrated passage dealing with the French peasants he wrote: 'In so far as millions of families live under economic conditions of existence that separate their mode of life, their interests and their culture from those of the other classes, and put them in hostile opposition to the latter, they form a class. In so far as there is merely a local interconnection among these smallholding peasants, and the identity of their interests begets no community, no national bond and no political organization among them, they do not form a class. They are consequently incapable of enforcing their class interests in their own name, whether through a parliament or through a convention. They cannot represent themselves, they must be represented.'[21] Marx, an urban intellectual if there ever was one, had little sympathy for the peasants. 'Small property and land', he wrote, 'is conditioned upon the premise that the overwhelming majority of the population is rural and that not the social, but the isolated labor predominates; that, therefore, in view of such conditions, the wealth and development of reproduction, both in its material and intellectual sides, are out of the question and with them the prerequisites of a rational culture.'[22] He was totally convinced of the absolute superiority of large-scale to peasant farming and believed that the victory of the former was inevitable.[23] Peasants, who could be both employer and employee, landowner and tenant, capitalist and worker – sometimes at the same time – could not be contained within his neat dialectic: they were assigned a place as suspect and unreliable allies of the urban proletariat, a judgment which was to have such profound consequences for the development of society in Russia and in the other peasant states of eastern Europe.

The most determined rearguard action against the forces of change and modernization was fought by the peasants in Russia. In 1905 about

100,000 noble families still owned nearly fourteen million acres of land in European Russia, while nearly twelve million peasant families owned only three times as much.[24] Following defeats in the Russo-Japanese War, a wave of revolution swept out of the towns to engulf the countryside, with both socialists and liberals supporting peasant demands for redistribution of the land. But the eternal peasant hopes – 'All the land here belongs to us really,'[25] one peasant leader told a British visitor in 1905 – were destroyed with the failure of the revolution.

During the revolution, Peter Stolypin (1862–1911) had attracted the attention of the tsar by his energetic suppression of peasant disturbances in Saratov province, of which he was then the governor. In 1906 he was made prime minister and carried out a series of agrarian reforms, which were designed to create a new class of more substantial peasant farmers (kulaks), to act as a more stable conservative force in the countryside. In 1907 remaining redemption payments were cancelled; three years later the legal ownership of scattered strips of land by the *mir* started to be replaced by individual ownership of consolidated farms; and the Peasant Land Bank, which had been established in 1882, expanded credit facilities for peasants to purchase land from the nobility.

These conservative reforms did not placate the mass of peasants who wanted a redistribution of all the land on a much more egalitarian basis. After the October Revolution Lenin, in need of food and soldiers from the countryside, was forced to abandon his opposition to private ownership of land and give way to peasant demands. In many parts of the country the peasants took over the estates of the nobility – and their possessions, too – splitting them up among themselves and also redistributing the land of wealthier kulaks. The Civil War brought anarchy to the Russian countryside, with Red Army detachments requisitioning food from peasants by force, serious famine and numerous peasant uprisings. Thousands of peasants in the southern Ukraine volunteered to serve under the black banners of that remarkable, but irresponsible, peasant guerrilla leader Nestor Makhno (1889–1935), who, like Pugachev and Razin before him, had aroused millenarian hopes in the Russian countryside. Far away from what Makhno called 'the smell of lying and betrayal' in the cities, he set up small agrarian communes, 'the happy germ of a new social life',[26] which peasants were free to join even if they were not anarchists like Makhno himself. But Makhno was

рена мира представляла
Сплошной кровавый кавардак.
Буржуям крови было мало, —
Подняли весь народ для драк.

Сносили многое солдаты,
Терпел безропотно народ,
Пока под грохот канонады
Вдруг не возник переворот.

Тогда настал для нас рассвет, —
Страною править стал Совет.

82 'All power to the Soviets!' A revolutionary poster which assigned to the peasantry a position of importance beside the urban proletariat and the Red Army.

betrayed by the Red Army. After he had beaten off attacks in the Ukraine by the White armies, his commanders were called to a conference with the Red Army in the Crimea in November 1920, where they were immediately seized and shot. Makhno himself escaped, eventually reaching Paris 'where he lived on, tuberculous, alcoholic, a bitter and lonely peasant who hated the city, until 1935'.[27]

These uprisings and the continuing grave shortage of food forced Lenin to make further concessions to the peasants. Under his New Economic Policy of 1921, compulsory grain deliveries were replaced by a tax in kind and peasants were given greater freedom to sell their produce on the market. This policy of encouraging free enterprise in the countryside was continued for some years after Lenin's death, until Stalin decided, under the first five-year plan, to submit agriculture forcibly to Marxist orthodoxy by collectivization, large-scale farming, the liquidation of the kulaks (a wide category which included all peasants who opposed his plans) and the domination of the countryside by the towns. With the tractor as the spearhead of his advance and the political police, the OGPU, to mop up all pockets of peasant resistance, Stalin tried to drive Russian agriculture into the modern age – a very necessary advance, but one which was made at enormous human cost and suffering, the true extent of which will probably never be known. There was widespread resistance to collectivization. The peasants fought back with knives and fire, killing officials, burning crops, and destroying millions of animals, which set Russian agriculture back even further. But, by the mid-1930s, the land of about twenty million peasant families had been consolidated into some 250,000 collective farms and four thousand large state farms. 'The collectivization of Russian peasant agriculture', writes its historian Volin, 'began with the horrors of mass deportation and ended with the ordeal of mass famine.'[28] It is estimated that during this process some five to five and a half million people died, mainly as a result of the famine of 1932–33.

Peasant resistance to collectivization was so great that even Stalin had to make some concessions by authorizing private peasant plots and the private ownership of some livestock. Although this was introduced only as a temporary measure, the peasants' non-cooperation with the collectives remained so great that private production assumed a more and more important part in Russian agriculture. By the late 1960s about one-third of all Russian agricultural output came 'from the peasant's exiguous private plot and private cattle'.[29] Stalin's policy of coercion produced immense changes in farm structure and a great increase in mechanization, but the full modernization of agriculture has remained one of the major problems of the Soviet state, and one which has helped to bring about the downfall of post-Stalin leaders from Malenkov to Khrushchev.[30]

Similar difficulties in bringing agriculture into the modern age were encountered elsewhere in eastern Europe and in the Balkans. With the dismemberment of the Austro-Hungarian Empire after the First World War, millions of peasants became nationals of new or expanded countries as the frontiers of Europe were withdrawn. The new governments faced the same problems of land hunger, poverty and relative lack of industrialization which, before the war, had forced thousands of peasants to leave their homes in Hungary, Poland, Galicia, Ruthenia, Moravia and Bohemia to labour as migrant workers on Junker estates in Prussia, large farms and estates in Lower Austria and on the Hungarian plains, and on sugar-beet farms in Sweden. During the last decades of the nineteenth century an increasing number of peasants emigrated: in 1907, the peak year for immigration into the United States before the First World War, only 200,000 came from western Europe, while another million came mainly from Austria-Hungary, the Balkans, Russia and Italy.[31] But even this massive emigration did very little to reduce the total of under-employed and landless in these vast undeveloped lands, with their primitive agriculture, where some 60 to 80 per cent of the total population in each country were still peasants or landless labourers who provided 50 to 60 per cent of the national income.[32] Huge estates still remained in many countries, particularly in Hungary and in Poland, creating a highly divisive society of rich and poor.

After the First World War, with the neighbouring example of Russia as a warning, practically all eastern governments introduced programmes for land reforms, which broke up some large estates and redistributed the land to peasant farmers who usually had to pay part of the compensation to landowners in instalments. Some of these reforms were introduced by the leaders of peasant parties, which had been formed around the turn of the century in many east European and Balkan countries. These leaders, not remote intellectuals from distant cities but the educated sons of peasants, imbued with the inter-war idea of the Green International in opposition to the Red International of the towns, tried unsuccessfully to create genuine peasant states instead of nations of peasants. One of the leading exponents of the idea of the Green International was the Bulgarian Alexander Stamboliski (1879–1923), leader of the Agrarian League from 1908. He hoped that Bulgaria, which was already a land of smallholders to a considerable extent, might become the basis for a movement which would unite all southern Slavs. After helping to bring about the abdication of King Ferdinand in 1918, Stamboliski became prime minister in the following year, ruling Bulgaria virtually as a dictator and seeking to promote peasant interests by shifting the main burden of taxation from the countryside to the towns. In Poland, Wincenty Witos (1874–1945) became leader of the peasant party, Piast, which had been formed in 1895, and was a deputy in the Austrian Reichsrat from 1911 to 1918. After the war he was prime minister of Poland three times between 1920 and 1926, when he introduced a programme of moderate land reform which, however, would have left many of the large estates intact. One of the staunchest defenders of the idea of the peasant state was Stjepan Radic (1871–1928), who became a journalist after studying at home and abroad, and then helped to found the Croatian Peasant Party in 1904. Believing that true democracy could only arise from below, he envisaged a confederation of Slav states, based on the potential economic and cultural strength of their respective peasantries, with villages sending representatives to regional councils, somewhat along Soviet lines.

These short-lived dreams ended in a nightmare of terror, exile and violence. One by one the peasant leaders fell, the victims of right-wing *coups*, landowners' intrigues and nationalist passions. In 1923, after a right-wing *coup* in Bulgaria, Stamboliski was shot, partly as a result of his agrarian policies but also because his *rapprochement* with Yugoslavia offended the Macedonian nationalists in Bulgaria. Three years later, Witos was overthrown after a military *coup* in Poland, led by Joseph Pilsudski, a former socialist general, who emerged from his retirement in 1926 as a conservative dictator. Witos fled later to Czechoslovakia, fearing that he would be rearrested after an illegal prison sentence had been quashed. In 1928 Radic, who had just come to an agreement with a Serbian democrat leader for the reorganization of Yugoslavia as a federal state, was shot in the National Assembly by a Serbian deputy and died of his wounds a month or so later.

The forces of reaction in eastern Europe, outside Russia, proved to be too strong not only for peasant parties but also for communists. In 1919, Bela Kun, a Hungarian who had been trained by the Bolsheviks in Russia, set up a communist republic in Hungary, but it was destroyed after a few short months by a counter-revolution of the right led by Admiral Horthy. Only in Czechoslovakia, that sad and ill-fated land, did a democratic state arise, which carried out successful land reforms and a programme of industrialization under the wise guidance of Thomas Masaryk and the diplomatic skill of Antonin Svehla, head of the Agrarian Party, who was prime minister during the infant years of the republic from 1922 to 1929.

Apart from Czechoslovakia, Yugoslavia and Rumania, land reform did not proceed very far in eastern Europe in the inter-war years, so that it is estimated that between two-thirds and three-quarters of the peasants were cultivating holdings insufficient to support their families on the eve of the Second World War.[33] Burdened by debts and heavy taxation, they tried to scrape a living from their small farms of between five and twelve acres using primitive tools and methods which had not changed for centuries. They were so poor that in the 1930s many of them were unable to buy 'matches, salt and oil – the three essentials of village life'.[34]

With the communist takeover in eastern Europe after the Second World War, the large estates were split up and the land was redistributed among the peasants. In East Germany, for example, most of the large farms of over 250 acres (over one-quarter of the total number in 1939) were split up between 1945 and 1946 and made into peasant farms of between twelve and a half and fifty acres. But, after a few years, a programme of collectivization was introduced, which was completed in East Germany by 1960, except in some areas which were said to be unsuitable for large-scale farming. As in Russia, at an earlier period, there was considerable peasant opposition. 'Agrarian leaders were usually untainted with collaboration and had large followings,' writes David Thomson. 'They stood for small private ownership, as encouraged by the initial redistributions of land in these states, and they were therefore the main opponents of communist collectivisation. They had to be ousted by fraud and force.'[35] Poland, which had always retained a strong nationalist and independent spirit, took a different line: collectivization was abandoned, so that most of the land is now in peasant hands again. Yugoslavia has also allowed private ownership of land since 1953, with an upper limit of twenty-five acres.

In spite of the very great differences which still exist between agriculture in eastern and western Europe, there has been a widespread acceleration in the rate at which the countryside has become dependent on the towns since the end of the Second World War, producing no less than a reversal of the traditional course of previous European history. The scythe has been hung up to rust and the reaper has been discarded, as the combine-harvester, which makes its own demand for farm engrossment and the uprooting of old field divisions, has increasingly taken over the harvest, not only in eastern Europe but also in the west. Between 1958 and 1970 the number of combine-harvesters increased sixfold in member-countries of the European Economic Community. Horses and oxen have become a much rarer sight on farms in north-west and central Europe: the number of tractors in West Germany almost doubled between 1960 and 1970. The milking-stool has been put up for sale with other bric-à-brac in antique shops as more milking-machines have been installed on farms. Engineers of the Bord na Móna have developed huge peat-cutting machines which slice up whole sectors of the Irish bogs into neat briquettes, some of which are used to generate electricity in the Irish peat-fuelled power-stations. Parts of the Camargue, on the Rhône delta in southern France, which was until recently one of the wildest parts of western Europe with its cowboys rounding up wild bulls and horses in the salty marshes and lagoons, have been transformed into rice-fields. Water from the Rhône has been taken along a canal to Languedoc to allow flowers and early vegetables to be grown in irrigated fields for distant markets. Dairy farming in the Swiss and Austrian Alps has been revitalized by the installation of plastic pipelines, which allow milk to be gravity-fed direct from the high summer pastures to the cheese-processing plants in the villages some three thousand feet below.

Practically all farmers have become increasingly dependent on a much greater energy input derived from fossil fuels, directly in the form of oil for tractors, transport and machinery, and indirectly in the forms of electricity for drying, heating and ventilating and of the chemical by-products of oil-cracking plants, such as fertilizers, insecticides, fungicides and herbicides. Scientific innovations have been increasingly applied in agriculture, from the development of new varieties of plants and the breeding of livestock to the control of weeds in the ground and pests in the air. In the more advanced countries of north-west Europe, some sectors of agriculture – particularly eggs, vegetables and the white meat trade – have been increasingly industrialized. About 80 per cent of eggs in England now come from laying flocks kept in individual wire cages in battery-houses, where the birds are fed and watered automatically, and the eggs are taken away on a conveyor belt or on a hand-pushed trolley. Many piggeries have also been automated. Chickens from broiler-houses and vegetables from the fields are marketed as frozen foods – a development introduced by Clarence Birdseye (1886–1956) in the United States in 1925, which, however, did not gain great popularity there or in Europe until after the Second World War.

The mechanization and industrialization of farming have allowed much greater quantities of food to be produced by a smaller labour force from smaller areas of land to feed the growing populations of the cities and the towns; but the full consequences of this dependence on non-rural resources have not yet been generally realized. Although the application of new methods to farming has greatly increased crop yields, the increase in the energy input from fossil fuels has risen proportionately faster than the food output measured in kilocalories. As a result of this change in farming methods, the price of produce has become linked with the price of fossil fuels and their by-products –

and their availability. Political decisions made in distant Arabian capitals now have a great effect upon the price that consumers in western Europe have to pay for their food. Workers in the towns can now hold the countryside to ransom, as was demonstrated in Northern Ireland during the strike organized by the Ulster Workers' Council in May 1974, when cuts in electrical power and a ban on petrol supplies had an immediate and devastating effect on many farmers, who had to slaughter thousands of broiler chickens after the ventilator fans stopped or pour milk down the drains through lack of transport. The countryside is less of a cushion for the towns – its traditional role through the ages. Furthermore, some scientists are concerned about the long-term effects of scientific methods on the soil, particularly the replacement of much ley farming by mono-culture, based upon intensive applications of chemical fertilizers, which may in some places already have brought about a deterioration in the soil structure, built up by careful husbandry over the course of many centuries. The drift away from the land has also created serious imbalances in the social structure of the countryside, with its increasingly aged or retired population. All efforts to restore more beneficial and intimate links between town and countryside, pioneered by Sir Ebenezer Howard (1850–1928) with his garden cities at Letchworth and Welwyn, Hertfordshire, have so far failed: the New Towns of Britain are a mockery of his ideas.

For the last hundred years European governments have increasingly intervened in agriculture, originally to protect larger farmers during the agricultural depression in the last quarter of the nineteenth century and, again, in the agricultural slump of the 1930s; to increase food production in the two world wars; and, finally, to provide bigger outputs from the farms in the post-war period. Since the end of the Second World War, individual governments have poured thousands of millions of pounds into the land, in structural alterations such as the consolidation of small farms into larger units, reafforestation, land clearance and irrigation; in social measures, such as early retirement pensions to encourage older peasants to leave the land; in market support by guaranteed prices and intervention policies; and in subsidies for fuels and fertilizers, scientific services and interest rates. In West Germany alone the bill came to DM 4,580 m. in 1972.

On the whole, governments have proved to be somewhat better taskmasters than their predecessors, particularly where they have contented themselves with providing advice, support and investment

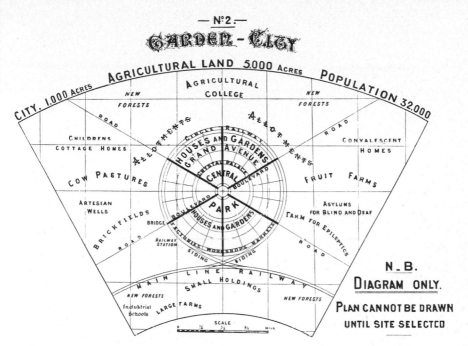

GARDEN-CITY

AGRICULTURAL LAND 5.000 ACRES   POPULATION 32.000

CITY. 1.000 ACRES

NEW FORESTS

AGRICULTURAL COLLEGE

NEW FORESTS

ROAD   ALLOTMENTS   ROAD

CHILDRENS COTTAGE HOMES

CONVALESCENT HOMES

CIRCLE RAILWAY

HOUSES AND GARDENS

GRAND AVENUE

CRYSTAL PALACE

CENTRAL PARK

COW PASTURES

FRUIT FARMS

ARTESIAN WELLS

BRICKFIELDS

BRIDGE

BOULEVARD

HOUSES AND GARDENS

FACTORIES WORKSHOPS MARKETS

RAILWAY STATION

SIDING   SIDING

ASYLUMS FOR BLIND AND DEAF

FARM FOR EPILEPTICS

ROAD

MAIN LINE RAILWAY

SMALL HOLDINGS

NEW FORESTS

Industrial Schools   LARGE FARMS

NEW FORESTS

SCALE

**N.B.
DIAGRAM ONLY.
PLAN CANNOT BE DRAWN
UNTIL SITE SELECTED**

83 Sir Ebenezer Howard's plan for new, beneficial links between town and country, as set out in *Garden Cities* (1902), was short-lived. Britain's New Towns bear little resemblance to the design shown above.

instead of trying to intervene directly between the farmer and the soil. But the problems are so vast – it is estimated that between one-third and one-half of the agricultural land in Europe needs to be reallocated or consolidated if the technical efficiency of both labour and capital is to be increased[36] – and the dangers of centralized control in such an individual activity as farming are so acute, that agriculture has remained the Achilles' heel of many governments both in the east and in the west. The attempt under the Common Agricultural Policy to create a free trade area in farm produce has brought about the greatest dissension in the European Economic Community and taken it at times to the verge of apparent disaster. Critics have concentrated their attention on the huge mountains of butter, bought up by governments at the intervention price, and kept in cold storage or sold at below cost price to the Russians, while butter continued to be sold at high prices in continental shops and supermarkets. But there

157

are far more fundamental defects. A large proportion of the lévies has gone, not so much on the greatly needed improvements in farm structures, but on subsidizing the exports of large, efficient farmers, particularly in France. The Common Agricultural Policy has strong historical links with continental policies in the 1880s. Modern efforts to find a solution to the age-old problems of investment in farming and the optimum size of holdings have been as tentative as they were in the past.

Progress in the post-war agricultural revolution has been as patchy as it was in the classic revolution of the eighteenth century. There are still great disparities in the proportion of each nation's labour force employed in agriculture – Greece, 45 per cent; Portugal, 31 per cent; Russia, 30 per cent; Spain, 29 per cent; Italy, 19 per cent; France, 13 per cent; Denmark, 11 per cent; West Germany, 8 per cent; Britain, 3 per cent – but in all countries there has been a gradual drift away from the land. The forces of the market have triumphed: in France, for example, 80 per cent of farm produce is now marketed against only 45 per cent ten years before. The Marxian analysis has been increasingly realized. In most of eastern Europe, the state, and in much of the west the bourgeoisie, 'has subjected the country to the rule of the towns. It has created enormous cities, greatly increased the urban population as compared with the rural, and thus rescued a considerable part of the population from the idiocy of rural life.'[37] The motor-car and the mass media have brought town visitors and ideas into the villages of Europe and have allowed country people to escape from their local environment, either in reality or in their imagination. The old-style European peasant, with his aim of self-subsistence, has already disappeared from many parts of Europe. Some have become worker-peasants, who leave their wives to run their small farms during the day while they work at some other job in a factory. Many more have left the countryside altogether and moved into the towns: their former homes have been put to new use by the bourgeoisie as weekend retreats or foreign holiday cottages. Others have settled in new lands on the far side of the world. A decreasing number of peasants still survive, eking out a poor existence on their small, unimproved farms, more commonly in the south of Europe than in other parts. As the present writer observed in 1960, change seemed scarcely to have touched the forbidding, boulder-strewn countryside of Beira Alta in Portugal with its blanketed shepherd boys, its wooden water-wheels, its ancient terraces held together by the vines, its oxen with their thatched head-coverings, and its rock-built houses, where the faces of women taking down the wooden shutters 'were framed darkly in the blank spaces like uncleaned Rembrandts'.[38] But even in that most backward region of Europe, there were many villages which had been deserted by their inhabitants, bringing to an end a way of life which had arisen ten thousand years or so before in the Middle East, where the wheat and barley, which grew wild, were cultivated and the goat and the sheep were probably first domesticated.

Throughout its long history, subsistence farming had left the farmer at the mercy – or the tyranny – of nature and the elements, and had usually provided so small a surplus that it was incapable of supporting a rich and free life for any but a privileged few. In spite of the great variations that could be found in individual villages and hamlets, and in different countries, it had led in very general terms to a polarized society, with lord and peasant locked in an increasingly hostile and suspicious relationship which contributed to their own inertia. The peasants, divided among themselves almost as much as they were from their masters, did not usually possess sufficient political and social strength to break their bonds, or a viable aim which could have sustained their freedom; while there was little incentive for the lords to change a system which so often provided them with a disproportionate share of the surplus wealth. On one side the system led to poverty, sloth and resignation, and hoarding by the more successful peasants; and, on the other side, to over-conspicuous consumption by prelates, lords and kings. As a result, investment remained negligible. The necessary third force to disturb this sometimes symbiotic relationship was lacking; even autocratic kings and tsars, in whom the Russian peasants put so much misplaced faith, could do relatively little, even where they wanted to.

The forces of the market did what no individuals could accomplish, and within a few centuries had succeeded in transforming the pattern of farming and the structure of society throughout much of Europe. Farming for the market was not new: it had existed in the Middle Ages and even earlier. For many centuries some basically subsistence farmers had been involved in it, and they had also had to depend on outside sources to supply some of their own needs, such as that for salt. There was never an exact dichotomy between market and subsistence farming. But, from the eighteenth century at least, there was a trend against the traditional, widespread emphasis on subsistence.

Towns created a self-sustaining pattern of growth. Their demand for food stimulated agricultural improvement; the bigger supplies allowed a larger population to be sustained in the towns, which could then absorb some of the redundant workers from the countryside. The lengthy transition from rural to urban living was neither smooth nor easy; the process was often unsynchronized, which produced some dreadful human suffering; but once it was well under way, it moved forwards jerkily and roughly with an irresistible force which dragged the countryside behind it at an increasingly rapid pace. The sickle had been used for the grain harvest since Neolithic times. It was not until the first half of the nineteenth century that it was largely replaced in England by the heavier, faster faghook and the scythe, which cuts grain crops some three to four and a half times more quickly than the sickle. It had taken many millennia for that simple change to be made; but, as the forces of the market increased in strength, within a century the scythe had been replaced by the horse-drawn reaper, then by the self-binder, and finally by the combine-harvester, without which the burgeoning urban populations of modern times could not be adequately fed.

The post-war revolution in agriculture has created new social and ecological problems of its own in the European countryside and has still failed to solve completely some of the traditional problems, such as the chronic instability of farm prices and the disparity in the living standards in town and country. The increasing dependence of the countryside on the towns has taken us into new uncharted seas which may contain hidden dangers. But agriculture has always depended on man's endeavours. If God created the world, much of the countryside has been shaped, for good or evil, by millions of unknown farmers over many centuries. Without their labour, much of Europe would still be covered by forest; terraces on southern hillsides would have tumbled; and the four main domesticated animals used for food would still run wild. Agriculture still demands close attention. If wheat was left to seed itself it would revert in no more than four years into a wild plant, as was shown in the Broadbalk Wilderness experiment. Investment remains the main key to agricultural progress. By pouring money into the land, particularly in the post-war period, European governments have already eliminated some of the worst legacies of the past, though many more still remain. The countryside is no less of an artefact than are the cities and the towns: we neglect it, or misuse it, at our peril.

BROADBALK WILDERNESS

LAST SURVIVING WHEAT PLANTS FOUND AUGUST 28th. 1886.

PART OF THE 39th. WHEAT CROP ON BROADBALK WAS LEFT TO SEED ITSELF DOWN AT THE HARVEST OF 1882.

NO CULTIVATION OF ANY KIND WAS GIVEN.

THE SPECIMENS BELOW WERE THE LAST PLANTS FOUND.

REFERENCES

I THE PEASANT WORLD

1 Peter Laslett, *The World we have Lost* (London, 1973), pp. 23–54.
2 James Harrington, *Oceana* (Heidelberg, 1924), p. 169.
3 F. Martini, *Das Bauerntum im deutschen Schrifttum von den Anfängen bis zum 16. Jahrhundert* (Halle, 1944), pp. 390–3.
4 Pitrim Sorokin and Carle C. Zimmerman, *Principles of Rural-Urban Sociology* (New York, 1929), p. 306.
5 Quoted in Roland Mousnier, *Peasant Uprisings* (London, 1971), p. 10.
6 Marc Bloch, *French Rural History* (London, 1966), p. 5.
7 Quoted in *ibid.*, p. 113.
8 Daniel Thorner, 'The Peasantry as an Economy' in Teodor Shanin (ed.), *Peasants and Peasant Societies* (Harmondsworth, 1973), p. 207.
9 Quoted in Michael Roberts, 'Queen Christina and the General Crisis of the Seventeenth Century' in *Past and Present* No. 22, 1962 (Oxford), p. 46.
10 C. A. Macartney, *Hungary: a short history* (Edinburgh, 1962), p. 31.
11 *Ibid.*, p. 62.
12 Dénes Sinor, *History of Hungary* (London, 1959), p. 141.
13 Quoted in A. W. B. Simpson, *An Introduction to the History of the Land Law* (Oxford, 1961), p. 6.
14 John Locke, *Two Treatises on Government* (London, 1821), p. 295.
15 Bloch, *op. cit.*, p. 128.
16 Julius Klein, *The Mesta: a study in Spanish economic history, 1273–1836* (Cambridge, Mass., 1920), pp. 424–8.
17 Quoted in Bloch, *op. cit.*, p. 188.
18 Karl Marx, *Capital* (Chicago, 1908), Vol. III, p. 933.
19 T. K. Derry, *A Short History of Norway* (London, 1968), p. 111.
20 Brian Fullerton and Alan F. Williams, *Scandinavia* (London, 1972), p. 43.
21 Mousnier, *op. cit.*, p. 228.
22 André J. Bourde, *The Influence of England on the French Agronomes, 1750–1789* (Cambridge, 1953), p. 38.
23 Laslett, *op. cit.*, p. 38.
24 B. H. Slicher van Bath, *The Agrarian History of Western Europe, A.D. 500–1850* (London, 1963), pp. 128–30.
25 Gerhard E. Lenski, *Power and Privilege* (New York, 1966), p. 283.
26 W. G. Hoskins, *The Midland Peasant: the economic and social history of a Leicestershire village* (London and New York, 1965).
27 *Ibid.*, p. 185.
28 *Ibid.*, p. 204.
29 Pierre Goubert, 'The French Peasantry of the Seventeenth Century: A Regional Example' in *Past and Present* No. 10, 1956 (Oxford), pp. 55–7.
30 *Ibid.*, p. 60.
31 *Ibid.*, p. 65.
32 Emmanuel Le Roy Ladurie, *Les Paysans de Languedoc* (Paris, 1966), 2 vols.
33 E. Estyn Evans, 'The Ecology of Peasant Life in Western Europe' in William L. Thomas Jr (ed.), *Man's Role in Changing the Face of the Earth* (Chicago, 1956), p. 223.
34 Quoted in Eric Kerridge, *The Farmers of Old England* (London, 1973), p. 57.
35 Derry, *op. cit.*, p. 17.
36 Walter Bacon, *Finland* (London, 1970), p. 84.
37 Quoted in Robert Bell (ed.), *Ancient Poems, Ballads, Songs of the Peasantry of England* (London, 1862), p. 224.
38 *Ibid.*, pp. 153–4.

II CHANGES IN AGRICULTURE

1 Eric Kerridge, *The Farmers of Old England* (London, 1973), p. 74.
2 Francis Bacon, *The Essays* (London, 1902), p. 88.

3 J. M. Houston, *The Western Mediterranean World* (London, 1964), p. 132.

4 Houston, *loc. cit.*

5 Philip K. Hitti, *History of the Arabs from the Earliest Times to the Present* (London, 1970), p. 528.

6 For a summary of the debate see C. T. Smith, *An Historical Geography of Western Europe before 1800* (London, 1967), pp. 191–259.

7 Lynn White Jr, *Mediaeval Technology and Social Change* (Oxford, 1962), pp. 72–3.

8 Julius Klein, *The Mesta: a study in Spanish economic history, 1273–1836* (Cambridge, Mass., 1920), p. 25.

9 René Dumont, *Types of Rural Economy: studies in world agriculture* (London, 1957), p. 210.

10 Thomas More, *Utopia* (London, 1973), p. 48.

11 Maurice Beresford, *The Lost Villages of England* (London, 1954), p. 166.

12 A. N. Duckham, *The Fabric of Farming* (London, 1958), p. 63.

13 White, *loc. cit.*

14 Adam Smith, *The Wealth of Nations* (London, 1950), Vol. I, p. 150.

15 Emmanuel Le Roy Ladurie, *Times of Feast, Times of Famine: a history of climate since the year 1000* (London, 1972), pp. 292–3.

16 P. C. J. A. Boeles, *Friesland tot de Elfde Eeuw* (The Hague, 1951), pp. 69–80.

17 White, *op. cit.*, p. 87.

18 B. H. Slicher van Bath, *The Agrarian History of Western Europe, A.D. 500–1850* (London, 1963), p. 297.

19 Sir Richard Weston, *A Discours of Husbandrie used in Brabant and Flanders* (London, 1650), p. 13.

20 B. H. Slicher van Bath, 'The Rise of Intensive Husbandry in the Low Countries' in Charles K. Warner (ed.), *Agrarian Conditions in Modern European History* (New York and London, 1966), p. 38.

21 Alma Oakes and Margot Hamilton Hill, *Rural Costume* (London and New York, 1970), pp. 222–9.

22 Peter Michelsen and Holger Rasmussen, *Danish Peasant Culture* (Copenhagen, 1955), pp. 48 and 53.

23 Slicher van Bath, *Agrarian History*, p. 176.

24 Colin Clark, *Population Growth and Land Use* (London, 1968), p. 152.

25 Fynes Moryson, *An Itinerary* (London, 1617), p. 97.

26 Basil Lubbock (ed.), *Barlow's Journal* (London, 1934), Vol. I, pp. 35–6.

27 Quoted in John Burnett, *A History of the Cost of Living* (Harmondsworth, 1969), p. 125.

28 Vilhelm Moberg, *A History of the Swedish People* (London, 1973), Part II, p. 47.

29 *Ibid.*, p. 44.

30 D. E. C. Eversley, 'Population, Economy and Society in D. V. Glass and D. E. C. Eversley (eds.), *Population in History: essays in historical demography* (London, 1965), p. 55.

31 Howard W. Haggard, *Devils, Drugs and Doctors* (London, n.d.), p. 219.

32 Quoted in Emmanuel Le Roy Ladurie, *Times of Feast, Times of Famine: a history of climate since the year 1000* (London, 1972), p. 69.

33 J. Meuvret, 'Demographic Crises in France from the Sixteenth to the Eighteenth Centuries' in Glass and Eversley, *op. cit.*, p. 519.

34 Alan Mayhew, *Rural Settlement and Farming in Germany* (London, 1973), p. 120.

35 Pierre Goubert, 'The French Peasantry of the Seventeenth Century: a regional example' in *Past and Present* No. 10, 1956 (Oxford), p. 70.

36 R. Zangheri, 'The historical relationship between Agriculture and Economic Development in Italy' in E. L. Jones and S. J. Woolf (eds.), *Agrarian Change and Economic Development: the historical problems* (London, 1970), p. 39.

163

37 Helen Douglas Irvine, *The Making of Rural Europe* (London, 1923), p. 57.

38 Fernand Braudel, *The Mediterranean and the Mediterranean World in the Age of Philip II* (London, 1972), Vol. I, p. 77.

III THE ENGLISH ACHIEVEMENT

1 J.D. Chambers and G.E. Mingay, *The Agricultural Revolution, 1750–1880* (London, 1966), p. 172.

2 H.J. Massingham, *Country Relics* (Cambridge, 1939), pp. 100–1.

3 See for example M.A. Havinden, 'Agricultural Progress in Open Field Oxfordshire' in *Agricultural History Review* Vol. IX, 1961 (Reading), pp. 73–83.

4 W.G. Hoskins, *The Midland Peasant: the economic and social history of a Leicestershire village* (London and New York, 1965), p. 67.

4 Eric Kerridge, 'Turnip Husbandry in High Suffolk' in W.E. Minchinton (ed.), *Essays in Agrarian History* (Newton Abbot, 1968), Vol. I, p. 143.

6 Adam Smith, *The Wealth of Nations* (London, 1950), Vol. I, p. 362.

7 G.E. Mingay, *English Landed Society in the Eighteenth Century* (London, 1963), p. 171.

8 Sir Stephen Edward de Vere, *Report on the Mount Trenchard Estate* (London, 1852).

9 Quoted in Reginald Nettel, *Sing a Song of England* (London, 1954), p. 96.

10 See J.D. Chambers, 'Enclosure and Labour Supply in the Industrial Revolution' in E.L. Jones (ed.), *Agriculture and Economic Growth in England 1650–1815* (London, 1967), pp. 94–127.

11 David Roden, 'Field Systems of the Chiltern Hills and the Environs' in A.R.H. Baker and R.A. Butlin (eds.), *Studies of Field Systems in the British Isles* (Cambridge, 1973), p. 373.

12 N.W. Pirie, *Food Resources Conventional and Novel* (Harmondsworth, 1969), p. 37.

13 W.G. Hoskins, *The Midland Peasant: the economic and social history of a Leicestershire village* (London and New York, 1965), p. 216.

14 N. Kent, *The Great Advantage of a Cow to the Family of a Labouring Man* (n.p., 1797).

15 M.K. Ashby, *Joseph Ashby of Tysoe* (Cambridge, 1961), p. 38.

16 Raymond Carr, 'Spain' in A. Goodwin (ed.), *The European Nobility in the Eighteenth Century* (London, 1967), p. 53.

17 Douglas Sutherland, *The Landowners* (London, 1968), pp. 33–4.

18 *Ibid.*, pp. 41–2.

19 *Gentleman's Magazine*, 21 June 1799 (London).

20 Kenneth Hudson, *Patriotism with Profit* (London, 1972), p. xii.

21 J.H. Plumb, *England in the Eighteenth Century* (Harmondsworth, 1955), p. 179.

22 J.L. and Barbara Hammond, *The Village Labourer* (London, 1948), Vol. I, pp. 184–5.

23 Chambers and Mingay, *op. cit.*, pp. 34–6.

24 See J.T. Ward and R.G. Wilson (eds.), *Land and Industry* (Newton Abbot, 1971), *passim*.

25 Paul Bairoch, 'Agriculture and the Industrial Revolution, 1700–1914' in C.M. Cipolla (ed.), *The Fontana Economic History of Europe* (London, 1973), Vol. 3, p. 491.

26 E.J. Hobsbawm and George Rudé, *Captain Swing* (London, 1961), pp. 262–3.

27 L.M. Cullen, 'Irish History without the Potato' in *Past and Present* No. 40, 1968 (Oxford), *passim*.

28 Colin Clark, *Population Growth and Land Use* (London, 1968), p. 84.

IV REPERCUSSIONS IN EUROPE

1 E.A. Wrigley, *Population and History* (London, 1969), p. 152.

2 *Ibid.*, p. 153.

3 Jean Marchand (ed.), *A Frenchman in England, 1784* (Cambridge, 1933), p. 208.

4 *Ibid.*, p. 196.

5 André J. Bourde, *The Influence of England on the French Agronomes, 1750–1789* (Cambridge, 1953), pp. 203–6.

6 *Ibid.*, pp. 189–90.

7 Ronald L. Meek, *The Economics of Physiocracy: essays and translations* (London, 1962), p. 128.

8 Joseph A. Schumpeter, *History of Economic Analysis* (London, 1955), p. 230.

9 Quoted in Alan Mayhew, *Rural Settlement and Farming in Germany* (London, 1973), pp. 121–2.

10 Giuliano Procacci, *History of the Italian People* (London, 1970), pp. 175–6.

11 Franco Venturi, *Italy and the Enlightenment* (London, 1972), p. 202.

12 *Ibid.*, p. 206.

13 Jerome Blum, *Lord and Peasant in Russia from the Ninth to the Nineteenth Century* (Princeton, N.J., 1961), pp. 334–5.

14 J. McManners, 'France' in A. Goodwin (ed.), *The European Nobility in the Eighteenth Century* (London, 1967), p. 32.

15 Klaus Epstein, *The Genesis of German Conservatism* (Princeton, N.J., 1966), pp. 208–10.

16 Stewart Oakley, *The Story of Denmark* (London, 1972), pp. 150–51.

17 T.K. Derry, *A Short History of Norway* (London, 1968), p. 118.

18 McManners, *loc. cit.*

19 Arthur Young, *Travels in France and Italy* (London and New York, 1934), p. 73.

20 *Ibid.*, p. 331.

21 A. Cobban, *The Social Interpretation of the French Revolution* (Cambridge, 1965), p. 51.

22 E. Labrousse, '1848–1830–1789: How Revolutions are Born' in F. Crouzet *et al.* (eds.), *Essays in European Economic History, 1789–1914* (London, 1969), pp. 3–4.

23 Gwynne Lewis, *Life in Revolutionary France* (London and New York, 1972), p. 66.

24 Klaus Epstein, *op. cit.*, pp. 211–12.

25 Quoted in Emil Ludwig, *Hindenburg* (London, 1935), p. 15.

26 A. Goodwin, 'Prussia' in Goodwin (ed.), *The European Nobility in the Eighteenth Century* (London, 1967), p. 99.

27 C. A. Macartney, 'Hungary' in *ibid.*, p. 129.

28 H. G. Shenk, 'Austria' in *ibid.*, p. 107.

29 Quoted in C. A. Macartney, *Hungary: a short history* (Edinburgh, 1962), p. 113.

30 William H. McNeill, *Europe's Steppe Frontier, 1500–1800* (Chicago and London, 1964), p. 130.

31 A. Bruce Boswell, 'Poland' in Goodwin (ed.), *op. cit.*, p. 167.

32 Quoted in Konstanty Grzybowski, 'Ten Centuries of Statehood – XII' in *Polish Perspectives* Vol. X, No. 3, March 1967 (Warsaw), p. 35.

33 Quoted in M. S. Anderson, *Peter the Great* (London, 1969), p. 27.

34 There is a well-documented account in Blum, *op. cit.*, from which many of the facts in the following paragraphs have been taken and are hereby gratefully acknowledged.

35 Raymond Carr, 'Spain' in Goodwin (ed.), *op. cit.*, p. 48.

36 H. V. Livermore, *Portugal: a short history* (Edinburgh, 1973), p. 131.

37 Quoted in H. Gille, 'The Demographic History of Northern European Countries in the Eighteenth Century' in *Population Studies* Vol. III, No. 1, June 1949 (Cambridge), p. 49.

38 Nicholas V. Riasanovsky, 'The Problem of the Peasant' in Wayne S. Vucinich (ed.), *The Peasant in Nineteenth-Century Russia* (Stanford, 1968), p. 264.

1 Thomas F. Glick, *Irrigation and Society in Medieval Valencia* (Cambridge, Mass. 1970), p. 15.

2 W.O. Henderson, *The Industrial Revolution on the Continent: Germany, France, Russia 1800–1914* (London, 1961), pp. 5–6.

3 John Burnett, *Plenty and Want* (Harmondsworth, 1968), pp. 200–1.

4 Emrys Jones, *Towns and Cities* (London, Oxford, New York, 1966), pp. 30–1.

5 Alexander Gerschenkron, *Bread and Democracy in Germany* (Berkeley and Los Angeles, 1943), p. 47.

6 Michael Tracy, *Agriculture in Western Europe* (London, 1964), p. 35.

7 Quoted in P. Lamartine Yates, *Food Production in Western Europe* (London and New York, 1940), p. 75.

8 *Outlines of a Plan for Providing a Settlement in South America.* Francis Place Collection, British Museum.

9 Philip Taylor, *The Distant Magnet* (London, 1971), p. 37.

10 Carlo M. Cipolla, 'Four Centuries of Italian Demographic Development' in D.V. Glass and D.E.C. Eversley (eds.), *Population in History: essays in historical demography* (London, 1965), p. 586.

11 Robert Wildhaber, introduction to H.J. Hansen, *European Folk Art in Europe and the Americas* (London, 1968), p. 8.

12 Tracy, *op. cit.*, p. 202.

13 Karl Dietrich Bracher, *The German Dictatorship* (London, 1971), p. 155.

14 Quoted in Yates, *op. cit.*, p. 448.

15 Doreen Warriner, *Economics of Peasant Farming* (London and New York, 1939), p. 42.

16 Jerome Blum, *Lord and Peasant in Russia from the Ninth to the Nineteenth Century* (Princeton, N.J., 1961), p. 438.

17 See *ibid.*, pp. 408–13.

18 Quoted in *ibid.*, p. 578.

19 Details may be found in G.T. Robinson, *Rural Russia under the Old Regime* (New York, 1932), pp. 64–93.

20 Quoted in D. Mitrany, 'Marx v. the Peasant' in T.E. Gregory and Hugh Dalton (eds.), *London Essays in Economics* (London, 1927), p. 352.

21 Karl Marx, 'The Eighteenth Brumaire of Louis Napoleon' in Marx and Engels, *Selected Works* (London, 1950), Vol. I, pp. 302–3.

22 Karl Marx, *Capital* (Chicago, 1908), Vol. III, p. 945.

23 *Ibid.*, p. 938.

24 Lazar Volin, *A Century of Russian Agriculture* (Cambridge, Mass., 1970), pp. 83–5.

25 Maurice Baring, *What I saw in Russia* (London, n.d.), p. 299.

26 Quoted in George Woodcock, *Anarchism* (Harmondsworth, 1963), p. 396.

27 *Ibid.*, p. 399.

28 Volin, *op. cit.*, p. 234.

29 Robert Conquest (ed.), *Agricultural Workers in the USSR* (London, 1968), p. 9.

30 *Ibid.*, p. 53.

31 Taylor, *op. cit.*, p. 48.

32 Warriner, *op. cit.*, p. 37.

33 Hugh Seton-Watson, *The East European Revolution* (3rd ed., London, 1956), p. 15.

34 H. Hessell Tiltman, *Peasant Europe* (London, 1936), p. ix.

35 David Thomson, *Europe since Napoleon* (London, 1962), p. 787.

36 Folke Dovring, 'The Transformation of European Agriculture' in M. Postan and H.J. Habbakuk (eds.), *Cambridge Economic History* (Cambridge, 1965), Vol. VI, Part II, pp. 630–1.

37 Karl Marx and Frederick Engels, 'The Communist Manifesto' in Arthur P. Mendel (ed.), *Essential Works of Marxism* (New York, 1961), p. 17.

38 Frank E. Huggett, *South of Lisbon* (London, 1960), p. 14.

BIBLIOGRAPHY

GENERAL

Aarne, Antti, *The Types of the Folktale*. Helsinki, 1964; New York, 1971
Baker, Alan R. H. (ed.), *Progress in Historical Geography*. Newton Abbot and
    New York, 1972
Boserup, Ester, *The Conditions of Agricultural Growth*. London, 1965; Chicago,
    1966
Chayanov, A. V., *The Theory of Peasant Economy*, ed. Daniel Thorner *et al.*
    Homewood, N.J., 1966
Clark, Colin, *Population Growth and Land Use*. New York, 1967; London,
    1968
——, and Margaret Haswell, *The Economics of Subsistence Agriculture*. London and
    New York, 1964
Coo, Joz. de, *De Boer in de Kunst van de 9e tot de 19e Eeuw*. Rotterdam, 1964
Crouzet, F., *et al.* (eds.), *Essays in European Economic History, 1789–1914*. London,
    1969; New York, 1970
Dovring, Folke, 'The Transformation of European Agriculture' in M. Postan and
    H.J. Habbakuk (eds.), *Cambridge Economic History*, Vol. VI, Part II.
    Cambridge, 1965
Duckham, A.N., *The Fabric of Farming*. London, 1958
Fleure, H.J., 'What is a Peasantry?' in *Bulletin of the John Rylands Library*
    XXI No. 2, 1937. Manchester
Franklin, S. H., *The European Peasantry: the final phase*. London, 1969
French, Mary, *Worm in the Wheat*. London, 1969
Fussell, G.E., *The Classical Tradition in West European Farming*. Newton Abbot
    and Cranbury, N.J., 1972
Galeski, B., *Basic Concepts of Rural Sociology*. Manchester and New York, 1972
Glass, D. V., and D. E. C. Eversley (eds.), *Population in History: essays in
    historical demography*. London and Chicago, 1965
Goodwin, A. (ed.), *The European Nobility in the Eighteenth Century*. London and
    New York, 1967
Gregor, Howard F., *Geography of Agriculture: themes in research*. Englewood
    Cliffs, N.J., 1970
Hansen, H.J. (ed.), *European Folk Art in Europe and the Americas*. London and
    New York, 1968
Hobsbawm, E.J., *Bandits*. New York, 1969; Harmondsworth, 1972
Hutchinson, Sir Joseph, *Farming and Food Supply: the interdependence of
    countryside and town*. Cambridge and New York, 1972
Jones, E. L., and S.J. Woolf (eds.), *Agrarian Change and Economic Development:
    the historical problems*. London and New York, 1970

Kosiński, Leszek, *The Population of Europe*. London, 1970
Laslett, Peter (ed.), *Household and Family in Past Time*. Cambridge and New York, 1972
Le Roy Ladurie, Emmanuel, *Times of Feast, Times of Famine: a history of climate since the year 1000*. New York, 1971; London, 1972
Mitrany, D., *Marx against the Peasant*, London, 1951; Chapel Hill, N.C., 1952
Moore, Barrington, *Social Origins of Dictatorship and Democracy: lord and peasant in the making of the modern world*. Boston, Mass., 1966; London, 1967
Morgan, W.B., and R.J.C. Munton, *Agricultural Geography*. London and New York, 1971
Oakes, Alma, and Margot Hamilton Hill, *Rural Costume*. London and New York, 1970
Parsons, Kenneth H., *et al.*, *Land Tenure*. Madison, Wisc., 1956
Pirie, N.W., *Food Resources Conventional and Novel*. Harmondsworth and San Francisco, 1969
Potter, J., *et al.* (eds.), *Peasant Society: a reader*. Boston, Mass., 1967
Redfield, R., *Peasant Society and Culture*. Cambridge and Chicago, 1956
Shanin, Teodor (ed.), *Peasants and Peasant Societies*. Harmondsworth, 1973
Smith, Louis P.F., *The Evolution of Agricultural Co-operation*. Oxford and New York, 1961
Sorokin, Pitrim, Carle Zimmerman and Charles J. Galpin, *A Systematic Source Book in Rural Sociology*. New York, 1965, 3 vols.
Thomas, William L., Jr, *Man's Role in Changing the Face of the Earth*. Chicago, 1956
Thompson, Stith, *Motif-Index of Folk Literature*. Copenhagen and Bloomington, Ind., 1955–58, 6 vols.
Ucko, Peter J., and G.W. Dimbleby (eds.), *The Domestication and Exploitation of Plants and Animals*. London and Chicago, 1969
Vansina, Jan., *The Oral Tradition*. Chicago, 1965; Harmondsworth, 1973
Warner, Charles K. (ed.), *Agrarian Conditions in Modern European History*. New York and London, 1966
Warriner, Doreen, *Economics of Peasant Farming*. London and New York, 1939
White, Lynn, Jr, *Mediaeval Technology and Social Change*. Oxford, 1962; New York, 1966
Wolf, Eric R., *Peasants*. Englewood Cliffs, N.J., 1966
——, *Peasant Wars of the Twentieth Century*. New York, 1970; London, 1971
Woodcock, George, *Anarchism*. New York, 1962; Harmondsworth, 1963
Wrigley, E.A., *Population and History*. London and New York, 1969

NORTH-WEST AND CENTRAL EUROPE

Abel, Wilhelm, *Agrarkrisen und Agrarkonjunktur in Mitteleuropa vom 13. bis zum 19. Jahrhundert*. Hamburg and Berlin, 1966
Agricultural History Review. Reading, 1953–
Ault, W.O., *Open-Field Farming in Mediaeval England: a study of village by-laws*. London and New York, 1972
Baker, A.R.H., and R.A. Butlin (eds), *Studies of Field Systems in the British Isles*. Cambridge and New York, 1973

Bloch, Marc, *French Rural History*. London and Berkeley, 1966
Blum, Jerome, *Noble Landowners and Agriculture in Austria, 1815–1848*.
  Baltimore, 1948
Bourde, André J., *The Influence of England on the French Agronomes, 1750–1789*.
  Cambridge and New York, 1953
Carsten, F. L., *The Origins of Prussia*. Oxford and New York, 1954
Chambers, J. D., and G. E. Mingay, *The Agricultural Revolution, 1750–1880*.
  London and New York, 1966
Cobban, A., *The Social Interpretation of the French Revolution*. Cambridge and
  New York, 1965
Connell, K. H., *Irish Peasant Society*. Oxford, 1968; New York, 1969
Cullen, L. M., *An Economic History of Ireland since 1660*. London, 1972; New
  York, 1973
Duby, Georges, *Rural Economy and Country Life in the Mediaeval West*. London
  and Columbia, S.C., 1968
Epstein, Klaus, *The Genesis of German Conservatism*. Princeton, N.J., 1966
Finberg, H. P. R. (ed.), *The Agrarian History of England and Wales*. Cambridge and
  New York, 1967
Folk Life. Cardiff, 1963–
Gerschenkron, Alexander, *Bread and Democracy in Germany*. Berkeley and
  Los Angeles, 1943
Goubert, Pierre, *Beauvais et le Beauvaisis de 1600 à 1730*. Paris, 1960, 2 vols.
Grant, I. F., *Highland Folk Ways*. London and Boston, Mass., 1961
Hammond, J. L. and Barbara, *The Village Labourer*. London, 1948, 2 vols.; New
  York, 1970
Hoskins, W. G., *The Midland Peasant: the economic and social history of a
  Leicestershire village*. London and New York, 1965
Johnson, Arthur H., *The Disappearance of the Small Landowner*, with an
  introduction by Joan Thirsk. Oxford, 1963
Jones, E. L. (ed.), *Agriculture and Economic Growth in England, 1650–1815*.
  London and New York, 1967
Kerridge, Eric, *The Agricultural Revolution*. London, 1967; New York, 1968
Laslett, Peter, *The World we have Lost*. London and New York, 1973
Lefebvre, Georges, *Les Paysans du Nord pendant la Révolution française*. Paris and
  Lille, 1924
Lindemans, P., *Geschiedenis van de Landbouw en België*. Antwerp and The Hague,
  1952, 2 vols.
Mayhew, Alan, *Rural Settlement and Farming in Germany*. London and New York,
  1973
Mills, Dennis R. (ed.), *English Rural Communities*. London, 1973
Mingay, G. E., *English Landed Society in the Eighteenth Century*. London, 1963
Nationale Coöperatieve Raad, *The Co-operative Movement in the Netherlands*.
  The Hague, 1956
Postan, M. M., *Essays on Mediaeval Agriculture and General Problems of the
  Mediaeval Economy*. Cambridge and New York, 1973
——, *The Mediaeval Economy and Society: an economic history of Britain in the
  Middle Ages*. London, 1972; Berkeley, 1973
Prebble, John, *The Highland Clearances*. London and New York, 1963

Russell, Sir E.J., *A History of Agricultural Science in Great Britain, 1620–1954*. London, 1966

Salaman, R.N., *The History and Social Influence of the Potato*, with a chapter on industrial uses by W.G. Burton. Cambridge and New York, 1949

Sharp, Cecil J., *English Folk Song*. Wakefield, Yorkshire, 1972

Slicher van Bath, B.H., *The Agrarian History of Western Europe, A.D. 500–1850*. London and New York, 1963

Tawney, R.H., *The Agrarian Problem in the Sixteenth Century*. London and New York, 1912

Thirsk, Joan, *English Peasant Farming: the agrarian history of Lincolnshire from Tudor to recent times*. London, 1957

Thompson, E.F.L., *English Landed Society in the Nineteenth Century*. London and Toronto, 1971

Tracy, Michael, *Agriculture in Western Europe*. London, 1964

Trow-Smith, Robert, *Life from the Land: the growth of farming in western Europe*. London, 1967

Ulster Folk Life. Belfast, 1955–

Wiese, H. and J. Bölts, *Rinderhaltung im Nordwesteuropäischen Küstengebeit vom 15. bis zum 19. Jahrhundert*. Stuttgart, 1966

Wimberly, Lowry Charles, *Folklore in English and Scottish Ballads*. New York, 1965

Yates, P. Lamartine, *Food, Land and Manpower in Western Europe*. London, 1960; New York, 1961

——, *Food Production in Western Europe*. London and New York, 1940

NORTHERN

Eskeröd, Albert, *Swedish Folk Art*. Stockholm, 1964

Folk-liv. Stockholm, 1939–

Jensen, E., *Danish Agriculture: its economic development*. Copenhagen, 1937

Mead, W.R., *Farming in Finland*. London, 1953; New York, 1954

Michelsen, Peter, and Holger Rasmussen, *Danish Peasant Culture*. Copenhagen, 1955

Ravnholt, Henning, *The Danish Co-operative Movement*. Copenhagen, 1947

Skrubbeltrang, Friedlev, *The Danish Folk High Schools*. Copenhagen, 1947

Vorren, O., and Ernst Manker, *Lapp Life and Custom*. London and New York, 1962

SOUTHERN

Braudel, Fernand, *The Mediterranean and the Mediterranean World in the Age of Philip II*. London and New York, 1972–73, 2 vols.

Dion, Roger, *Histoire de la vigne et du vin en France des origines au XIXᵉ siècle*. Paris, 1959

Dominguez Ortiz, A., *La Sociedad española en el siglo XVIII*. Madrid, 1955

Glick, Thomas F., *Irrigation and Society in Mediaeval Valencia*. Cambridge, Mass., 1970

Houston, J.M., *The Western Mediterranèan World*. London, 1964

Klein, Julius, *The Mesta: a study in Spanish economic history, 1273–1836*. Cambridge, Mass., 1920

Le Roy Ladurie, Emmanuel, *Les Paysans de Languedoc*. Paris, 1966, 2 vols.

Venturi, Franco, *Italy and the Enlightenment*. London and New York, 1972

Viñas Mey, Carmelo, *La reforma agraria en España en el siglo XIX*. Santiago, 1933

Walcot, P., *Greek Peasants, Ancient and Modern*. Manchester and New York, 1970

EAST AND BALKANS

Blum, Jerome, *Lord and Peasant in Russia from the Ninth to the Nineteenth Century*. Princeton, N.J., 1961

Conquest, Robert (ed.), *Agricultural Workers in the USSR*. London and New York, 1968

Dunn, Stephen P. and Ethel, *The Peasants of Central Russia*. New York, 1967

McNeill, William H., *Europe's Steppe Frontier, 1500–1800*. Chicago and London, 1964

Radkey, Oliver H., *The Agrarian Foes of Bolshevism*. New York and London, 1962

Smith, R.E.F., *The Enserfment of the Russian Peasantry*. Cambridge and New York, 1968

Tiltmann, H. Hessell, *Peasant Europe*. London, 1936

Tomasević, Jozo, *Peasants, Politics and Economic Change in Yugoslavia*. Stanford and London, 1955

Trouton, R., *Peasant Renaissance in Yugoslavia, 1900–1950*. London and New York, 1952

Venturi, Franco, *Roots of Revolution: a history of populist and socialist movements in nineteenth-century Russia*. London and New York, 1960

Volin, Lazar, *A Century of Russian Agriculture*. Cambridge, Mass., 1970

Vucinich, Wayne S. (ed.), *The Peasant in Nineteenth-Century Russia*. Stanford, 1968

(In view of the width of the topic, this bibliography has been restricted to a small core of mainly modern works, most of which were written in English or have been translated into that language. Many of these books contain extensive bibliographies of both English and foreign works, which will enable those who are interested in a particular aspect of the general topic to read on.)

LIST OF ILLUSTRATIONS

Klaes Molenaer (c. 1630–76). Museum Boymans-van Beuningen, Rotterdam

26 *The Young Bull*. Painting by Paulus Potter; 1647. Mauritshuis, The Hague

27 Peasant housing near Amboise. Drawing by Lambert Doomer (1623–1700). Louvre

28 Landscape with hut. Detail of painting by Jacob van Ruisdael (c. 1628–82). Kunsthalle, Hamburg

29 Peasant family. Painting by Giacomo Cernti (active 1720–50). Private collection

30 Soldiers plundering a village. Detail of tapestry *Art of War*, after a design by Lambert de Hondt; c. 1725. Victoria and Albert Museum

31 *The Ex Voto*. Painting by Alphonse Legros (1837–1911). Musée des Beaux-Arts, Dijon

32 Peasants at their meal. Fresco by Giovanni Domenico Tiepolo; 1757. Villa Valmarana, Vicenza

33 Enclosure petition to the House of Lords for Hadleigh parish; 1728. Record Office, House of Lords

34 Unenclosed field near Cambridge (detail) from *Cantabrigia Illustrata* by D. Loggan; 1690

35 *The Lincolnshire Ox*. Painting by George Stubbs (1724–1806). Walker Art Gallery, Liverpool

36 Jethro Tull's seed-drill. Eighteenth-century print. Science Museum, London

37 View of Hampton Court, Herefordshire. Detail of painting by Leonard Knyff; c. 1700. Photo courtesy of Sabin Galleries Ltd, Cork Street, London

38 *The Faggot Gatherers*. Detail of watercolour by Paul Sandby (1725–1809). Royal Library, Windsor Castle. Reproduced by gracious permission of H.M. Queen Elizabeth II

39 Surveyors at work. Detail from Henlow Enclosure Award Map, watercolour by J.

Goodman Maxwell; 1798. County Record Office, Bedford

40 *The Reapers*. Painting by George Stubbs (1724–1806). Upton House (National Trust)

41 *Mr and Mrs Andrews*. Painting by Thomas Gainsborough; c. 1748. Tate Gallery

42 Sheep-shearing at Woburn. Painting by George Garrard (1760–1826). Woburn Abbey Collection. Reproduced by permission of His Grace the Duke of Bedford

43 Man caught in a trap. Watercolour. Museum of English Rural Life, Reading

44 Bread riot, from *Looking Glass*; 1830. British Library

45 *Seed-Time*. Painting by John Frederick Herring, Senior; 1854. Victoria and Albert Museum

46 Summer and autumn. Popular print published at Orléans; late eighteenth century. Bibliothèque Nationale

47 Thomas Coke, Earl of Leicester, and his sheep. Painting by Thomas Weaver; c. 1800. Holkham Hall

48 Arthur Young. Drawing by George Dance; 1794. National Portrait Gallery, London

49 Shepherds of Les Landes from *Costumes des Provinces Françaises* by Grasset Saint-Sauveur; 1797. Victoria and Albert Museum

50 *Die Bittschrift*. Painting by Adolf von Menzel (1815–1905). Schloss Hohenzollern. Photo: Staatsbibliothek

51 Danish dairy c. 1880. Watercolour by R. Christiansen; 1919. Landbrugsmuseet, Lyngby

52 *Peasants Begging*. Etching by J. J. Boissieu; 1780. Bibliothèque Nationale

53 Peasant carrying on his back the clergy and the nobility. French popular print; 1789. Musée Carnavalet

54 Building a road. Detail of painting by Joseph Vernet; 1774. Louvre

high farming 83
Highland Society 80
high society 9, 15–21, 28–9, 44, 54, 87–8; see also nobility
Hirzel, Hans Kaspar 94
Hitler, Adolf 6, 143
Holstein 106
Holt, Alfred 130
horses 40, 43, 154
Hoskins, W. G. 31, 69, 75–6
Houston, J. M. 39
Howard, Sir Ebenezer 156
Hundred Years War 12
Hungary 6, 16, 88, 107, 137, 153
hunting 24, 74, 80, 100

Iberian peninsula 58; see also Spain, Portugal
industry 83, 122–4
infield-outfield system 37, 68
inflation 18, 27
intensive cultivation 50, 53, 69
investment 27, 45, 52, 61–3, 66, 70, 126, 158
Ireland 33, 35, 57, 68, 80, 84–5, 139–40, 156
irrigation 39–40, 45–8, 61–2
Italy 11, 26, 35, 37, 41, 45, 52, 61–3, 66, 94, 112–13, 115, 124, 134, 137, 141

Joseph II 107
Junkers 106, 132, 137
Jutland 53

Kerridge, Eric 37, 69
King, Gregory 23
Klein, Julius 21, 40
Kötter 31
Kropotkin, Prince Peter 148
kulaks 149–50
Kun, Bela 153

labour services 11, 16, 18–20, 97–8, 106–7, 110, 145
Labourers' Revolt (1830) 84
laboureurs 32, 99
Landes, Les 90, 91
landless 14, 72, 75, 98–100, 121, 139, 152

land reclamation 11, 45–8, 61–2, 90, 92
land reform 152–3
land shortage 11, 14–15, 119, 121, 151
land tenure 10–11, 23–7, 62–3, 113–14, 151–3, 156–7; Austria 107; Denmark 96–8; England 18–20, 73–8; France 20–1, 95, 104; Germany 95, 106; Russia 110–11, 145–6, 149
Lapps 43
La Rochefoucauld, François de 89–90
Laslett, Peter 9
Latimer, Bishop 30
Laval, Gustav de 135
Lawes, Sir John Benet 126
leases 11, 19, 62, 71–2, 102
Lefebvre, Georges 100
Leicester, Earl of 65, 79
Leicester sheep 67, 80
Lenin, V. I. 149–50
Leopold II 107, 113
Le Roy Ladurie, Emmanuel 32, 45
leys 50–1, 69
Liancourt, Duc de 89
Liebig, Justus von 126
livestock farming 23, 30, 37, 40–4, 50–3, 66–7, 79–80, 130, 135, 155
Livonia 145
Locke, John 18
Lofthus, Christian 98–9
Longhorn cattle 67
Low Countries 46–53, 69; see also Belgium, Flanders, Netherlands

Macartney, C. A. 107
Mafia 138
maize 60–1
Makhno, Nestor 149–50
manorial system 18–20
manouvriers 31, 99
mantraps 80, 81
maquis 23
Marggraf, Andreas 92
Maria Theresa 107, 113
Marie Antoinette 90
market, influence of 52, 71, 83, 119, 124–6, 159–60
marling 66
Marx, Karl 26, 148